The Customer Loyalty Audit

A Seven-Step Audit to Determine how Well-Equipped You Are to Win and Retain Customer Loyalty

Keki R. Bhote
Keki R. Bhote Associates

An imprint of **PEARSON EDUCATION**

London • New York • San Francisco • Toronto • Sydney
Tokyo • Singapore • Hong Kong • Cape Town • Madrid • Paris • Milan • Munich • Amsterdam

PEARSON EDUCATION LIMITED
Head Office:
Edinburgh Gate
Harlow CM20 2JE
Tel: +44 (0)1279 623623
Fax: +44 (0)1279 431059

London Office:
128 Long Acre, London WC2E 9AN
Tel: +44 (0)207 447 2000
Fax: +44 (0)207 240 5771
Website: www.business-minds.com

———————————

First published in Great Britain in 2000

© Cambridge Strategy Publications Ltd 2000

Published in association with
Cambridge Strategy Publications Ltd
39 Cambridge Place
Cambridge CB2 1NS

The right of Keki R. Bhote to be identified as Author
of this Work has been asserted by him in accordance
with the Copyright, Design and Patents Act 1988.

ISBN 0 273 64935 3

British Library Cataloguing in Publication Data
A CIP catalogue record for this book can be obtained from the British Library

All rights reserved; no part of this publication may be reproduced, stored
in a retrieval system, or transmitted in any form or by any means, electronic,
mechanical, photocopying, recording, or otherwise without either the prior
written permission of the Publishers or a licence permitting restricted copying
in the United Kingdom issued by the Copyright Licensing Agency Ltd,
90 Tottenham Court Road, London W1P 0LP. This book may not be lent,
resold, hired out or otherwise disposed of by way of trade in any form
of binding or cover than that in which it is published, without the
prior consent of the Publishers.

10 9 8 7 6 5 4 3 2 1

Typeset by Pantek Arts, Maidstone, Kent
Printed and bound in Great Britain

The Publishers' policy is to use paper manufactured from sustainable forests.

THE CUSTOMER LOYALTY AUDIT

CONTENTS

Part 1: Transition from Customer Satisfaction to Customer Loyalty 1

What Will You Get from this Audit? 3

Customer Satisfaction — Necessary But Not Sufficient 5

Customer Loyalty: the Ultimate Challenge 11

Customer Differentiation: Focus on "Core" Customers 17

The Ten Inviolate Principles of Customer Loyalty 21

Part 2: A Seven-Step Audit for Attaining and Maintaining Customer Loyalty 31

Step 1: Top Management Commitment and Involvement 33

Step 2: Internal Benchmarking — Establishing a Baseline 37

Step 3: Determining Customer Requirements 45

Step 4: Assessing the Capabilities of Competition 53

Step 5: Measuring Customer Satisfaction and Customer Loyalty 57

Step 6: Analyzing Customer and Competitive Feedback 65

Step 7: Continuous Improvement 73

Conclusion 81

References 82

Part 3: The Audit Process 85

Staffing the Audit Team 87

Creating an Audit Project Plan 89

Laying the Groundwork for the Audit 91

Analyzing Audit Results 93

Sharing Audit Results 97

Writing Effective Audit Reports 99

Dealing with Resistance to Recommendations 103

Building an Ongoing Audit Program 107

Part 4: Implementing a Customer Loyalty Audit: Questions and Checklists 109

Step 1: Top Management Commitment and Involvement 111

Step 2: Internal Benchmarking — Establishing a Baseline 113

Step 3: Determining Customer Requirements 119

Step 4: Assessing the Capabilities of Competition 123

Step 5: Measuring Customer Satisfaction and Customer Loyalty 125

Step 6: Analyzing Customer and Competitive Feedback 131

Step 7: Continuous Improvement 135

Part 1

TRANSITION FROM CUSTOMER SATISFACTION TO CUSTOMER LOYALTY

This audit is structured in four parts. Parts 1 and 2 examine the process of carrying out a customer loyalty audit. Part 3 looks at the audit process itself and provides a framework that addresses some of the logistical and process requirements of conducting an audit. Part 4 comprises a series of questions based on the seven steps in Part 2. These questions are designed to help you plan and implement your audit in a straightforward and practical manner.

THE CUSTOMER LOYALTY AUDIT

WHAT WILL YOU GET FROM THIS AUDIT?

The US Office of Consumer Affairs conducted exit surveys of 200 customers of a well-known Washington retailer.[1] It asked for responses on a range from very satisfied, moderately satisfied, moderately dissatisfied to very dissatisfied.

The results showed 54 percent of respondents who said they were very satisfied, and 46 percent who were either moderately satisfied, moderately dissatisfied or very dissatisfied. When this latter group was asked whether they had a specific complaint about something in the store, all of them did! Yet none of them had complained to the store. When asked why, the reply was they expected mediocre service and they did not believe anything would be done even if they complained — an indictment of the sorry state of the service industry.

The REL Consulting Group,[2] in a survey of Fortune 500 companies on customer retention and corporate profitability, reported 69 percent who felt a 5 percent customer defection rate would significantly affect profits. However, only one in six companies use customer retention as a measure to increase profitability.

This audit will offer more examples of companies without customer satisfaction as a key corporate objective. And most of those with this as a target have not gone the extra mile to "mine the gold" of real profit enhancement, by focusing on customer loyalty. To paraphrase an expression in mathematics, customer satisfaction is a necessary but not sufficient condition for an enterprise. Or, to put it even more succinctly, in the words of quality guru Dr. W. Edwards Deming: "A merely satisfied customer will go elsewhere when a competitor cuts its price."

Objectives

This audit will detail:

- A clear picture of why customer satisfaction in so-called enlightened companies is inadequate for achieving true competitive advantage.

- The importance of graduating from mere customer satisfaction to customer loyalty and lifelong customer retention.

The Customer Loyalty Audit

- How to differentiate between various groups of customers and focus on "core" customers, who constitute less than 20 percent by number but over 80 percent by sales.

- The inviolate principles of customer loyalty.

- A seven-step roadmap for attaining and maintaining customer loyalty, along with audits by which a company can assess the effectiveness of its customer loyalty at each step.

Benefits

Concentration on the methods described in this audit will enable a company to:

- Not only reduce the defection rate of its customers, but actually increase its retention rate.

- Convert one-time customers into lifelong customers, not only for a specific product but for the company's entire portfolio of product offerings.

- Achieve significant profit improvement — 50 percent and more — by concentrating on customer loyalty, rather run-of-the-mill approaches such as cost reduction or market share.

- Grow twice as fast,[3] charge 10 percent more and enhance return on investment by a factor of 2:1 — much more than the average company.

- Turn customer service departments into significant profit centers, and earn up to 400 percent return on investment in such departments.

- Make employee empowerment real instead of just another non-productive fad or slogan.

CUSTOMER SATISFACTION — NECESSARY BUT NOT SUFFICIENT

A recent *Fortune* magazine and Forum Corporation study found the following:

- Satisfied customers will tell an average of five other people about their positive experiences with a company's product or service.

- The average dissatisfied customer, however, will tell nine other people about their negative experiences.

- 13 percent of dissatisfied customers will broadcast their unhappiness with a company's product or service to 20 others.

- And, worst of all, 98 percent of dissatisfied customers never complain — they just switch to a competitor.

A Customer Commitment Survey

Learning Dynamics Inc.[4] recently conducted a customer commitment survey among a large number of companies. Its findings were:

- Only 57 percent rate meeting customer needs as their No. 1 priority.

- In 62 percent of companies, not everyone is aware of what customers do with their product or service.

- In 17 percent of companies, not even salespeople talk to customers; nor do 22 percent of senior management, 29 percent of marketing and 67 percent of R&D personnel.

- Only 60 percent base their competitive strategy on attention to customer needs.

- Fewer than half of new products and services are developed or improved based on customer suggestions and complaints, despite an MIT study indicating 80 percent of technological innovations — and the best innovations — come from customers.

- 12 percent of companies use no formal methods to determine customer wants.

- 13 percent have no one in their organization to represent the customer's point of view or act as the customer's advocate.

- 62 percent do not consider customer satisfaction a top priority.

- Only 3 percent rank customer satisfaction No. 1 in determining senior managers' compensation.

These are grim statistics. A company without a focus on customer satisfaction will not even qualify for the finals in world-class competition, despite its attention to price and cost reduction, technology, product quality or all three put together. And if it persists in paying marginal attention to the customer, it is likely to end up on the ash-heap of corporate history.

Why Companies Don't Focus on Customer Satisfaction

There are several reasons for corporations not paying sufficient attention to customers and their satisfaction:

- Companies have little knowledge or conviction about the main objective of suppliers being to create and nurture satisfied, repetitive and loyal customers who have received added value from their suppliers.

- Companies believe they are in business to make products or render services. But they seldom think they are in business to make satisfied, loyal, repetitive customers.

- This limited horizon extends to employees as well. Employees label themselves in terms of their professions or tasks, but almost never as customer satisfiers.

- Many employees feel too removed from customers, not recognizing they are links in a chain of customers, with the next operation as the immediate customer[5] and the external customer at the end of the chain.

- Much too often products are developed by listening to the "voice of management" or the "voice of the engineer," not the all-important "voice of the customer." In fact, management and engineers believe they know more about what customers want than the customers themselves!

- Company policies and procedures are designed for control and command, regardless of whether such policies mean anything to customers or — worse — can cause customer dissatisfaction.

- Customer contact employees — those front-line troops who interface frequently with customers — are not given authority to go beyond company policy in accommodating customer concerns and complaints and diffusing their anger with adjustments, compensation, etc. The trained "smile" for customers, assiduously taught to employees, is pathetic in its inadequacy.

- You obviously can't have happy customers without happy, productive employees. But the reason companies have indifferent, unmotivated employees has far less to do with the employees than with their over-bearing, dictatorial, short-sighted management.

- Departmental walls and organization boxes often promote competition between functions jockeying for power instead of cross-functional teamwork focused on customer needs and satisfaction.

Truly Satisfying Customers

Some progressive companies *do* pay close attention to their customers and achieve a high level of customer satisfaction. They have the following common characteristics:

They let their customers define their own criteria for generating enthusiasm

Figure 5 (page 26) depicts a network of various elements combining in the customer's mind to produce enthusiasm. These are not all equally important. While a company must achieve a minimum level of satisfaction for each element, it must concentrate on the elements the customer considers especially important and produce true value.

A few years ago UPS concentrated on fast delivery, feeling it was of paramount importance to its customers. It even redesigned the seats in its delivery vans to enable the drivers to get out faster! But sales still sagged. UPS discovered customers really wanted to interface with its harried drivers, ask questions and seek guidance. It then allowed drivers to spend more time with customers and even provided financial incentives to them when they generated more business. As a result, sales and profits shot up.

Varian Associates concentrated on the quality of its products. "All of our quality-based charts went up, but everything else went down," lamented Richard M. Levy, executive vice president for quality. Customer concerns took a back seat and Varian went from a profit gain to a profit loss. A massive effort had to be undertaken to improve customer satisfaction and restore Varian to profitability.

McDonald's, one of the best managed and most profitable companies in the world, concentrates on what its customers most want — consistent and uniform quality of its food in every country where it operates, at reasonable prices and without waiting.

Differentiating the customer base to focus on profitable customers

Not all customers are equally important or equally profitable to a company. The section on customer differentiation (pages 17–20) details a segmentation of customers between "core" customers — who constitute less than 20 percent by number but over 80 percent by sales — and others, who need not receive concentrated attention or may even be candidates for termination.

A few food chains are concentrating on their core customers, using data from computer systems to send them coupons on their favorite purchases and encouraging them to return to the same stores.

Federal Express developed a whole new business out of customers who wanted faster mail delivery and were willing to pay more than 10–20 times the price of the regular US postal service.

Investment in training and imaginative systems

Successful companies invest heavily in training and education for their employees. But such training should be focused on satisfying customer needs and not frittered away on general-purpose training or training not implemented on the job.

General Electric, as an example, has an extensive employee selection process, which profiles and screens candidates. Once hired, new employees are given an intensive training program about the needs of GE's customers. The company's answer center in Kentucky alone responds to three million calls each year and resolves 90 percent of customer inquiries on the first call.

Motorola started a comprehensive training process 16 years ago, when 1.5 percent of its payroll was used to fund the training budget. That promising start has now been institutionalized into a Motorola University, expending 5 percent of payroll and a minimum training of 40 hours a year for all its employees. The focus is on customer satisfaction, quality and cycle time.

Employees must also have access to sufficient information and authority to render customer service. American Express uses the Authorizer's Assistant, an artificial intelligence-based support software, to assist representatives in approving cardholder purchases quickly and efficiently.

Service responsiveness over quality and technology

A recent study[6] in the engineered components and subsystems industry asked the question: "What makes a supplier ideal?" in the eyes of its key customers. The results (Table 1) showed the *how* of service was twice as important as the *what* of the product. Within the product category, quality/reliability was twice as important as technology; and within the service category, responsiveness was five times as important as delivery and timing. This "emotion quotient" (EQ) is highlighted by Karen Boylston, director at the Center for Creative Leadership.[7] She says customers are telling businesses: "I don't care if every member of your staff graduated with honors from Harvard, Stanford and Wharton. I will take my business and go where I am understood and treated with respect."

**TABLE 1
WHAT MAKES A SUPPLIER IDEAL?**

PRODUCT		
• Quality/reliability		20.3%
• Technology		10.6%
	Sub-Total	30.9%
SERVICE		
• Delivery and timing		10.1%
• Responsiveness		55.2%
	Sub-Total	65.3%
OTHER		3.8%
	Total:	100%

Summary

Companies neglecting customer satisfaction do so at their own peril. But, as the next section will show, customer satisfaction, important though it may be, is not enough. For a company to achieve world-class status, it must graduate to customer loyalty.

CUSTOMER LOYALTY: THE ULTIMATE CHALLENGE

According to conventional wisdom, supposedly learnt from the Japanese, if you assure customer satisfaction profits will take care of themselves. Flying in the face of this conventional wisdom, however, is a recent survey conducted by the renowned Juran Institute. This found the following:

- 90 percent of top managers from over 200 of the largest corporations in the US claimed "maximizing customer satisfaction maximizes profitability and market share."

- Yet fewer than 30 percent were confident economic value had been added as a result of their customer satisfaction efforts.

- And fewer than 2 percent were able to measure a bottom-line improvement from documented increases in levels of customer satisfaction.

"It's Customer Loyalty — Stupid"

During the 1992 US presidential election campaign, the Clinton slogan was: "It's the economy — stupid." The economy was foremost in the minds of US voters. Similarly, customer loyalty rather than customer satisfaction is now the dominant key to business success.

Customer loyalty means customers are so delighted, so excited, with a company's products or services they become enthusiastic word-of-mouth advertisers. Further, they will extend their loyalty not only to the particular product or service but to the organization's whole portfolio of products and services for the better part of their lifetime — achieving both brand loyalty and longevity.

Figure 1 shows the poor correlation between customer satisfaction and customer loyalty across a broad spectrum of industries. In some consumer goods businesses, the percentage of satisfied customers is in the 90 to 95 percent range, but their loyalty is less than 50 percent. In sharp contrast, Figure 2 depicts the strong correlation between customer loyalty, as measured through repurchases (retention rates), and profitability.

THE CUSTOMER LOYALTY AUDIT

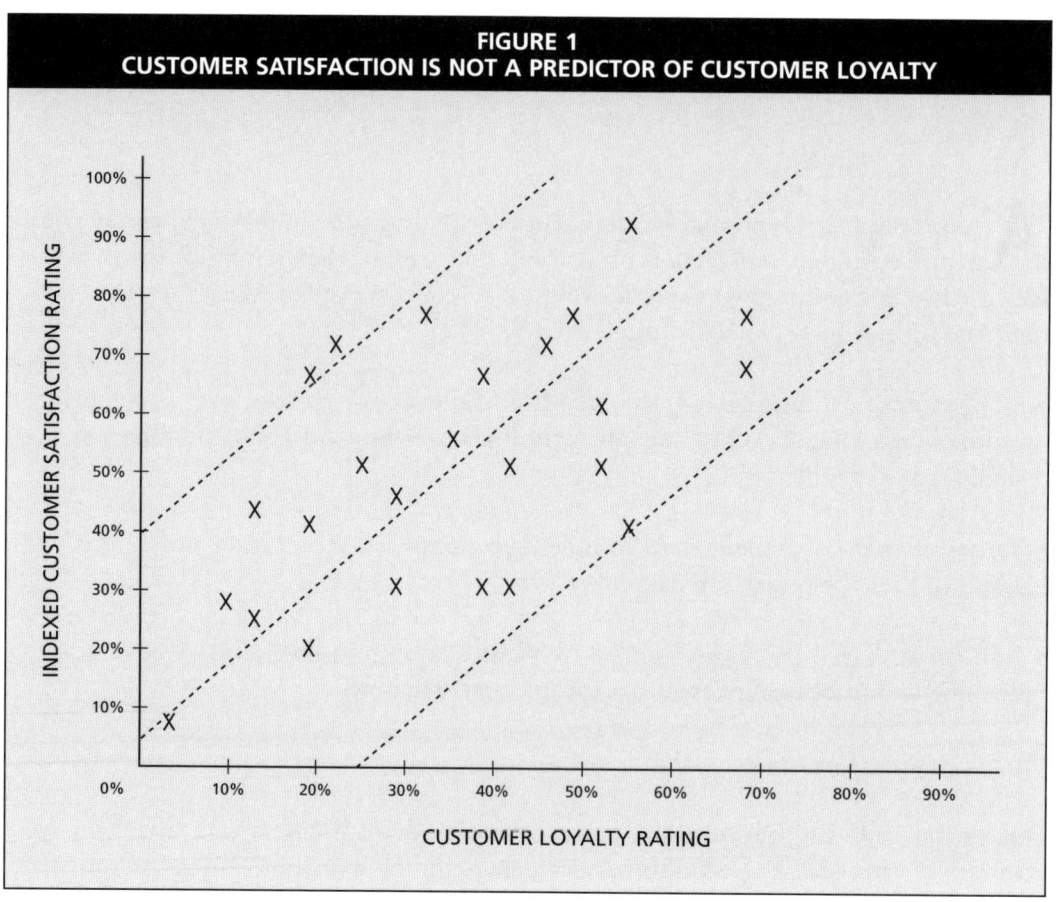

FIGURE 1: CUSTOMER SATISFACTION IS NOT A PREDICTOR OF CUSTOMER LOYALTY

Customer Loyalty — the New Testament

Figure 2 underlines the main business reason why the old testament of mere customer satisfaction must give way to the new testament of customer loyalty and retention. It is profit, profit and more profit. Business experts and academicians see customer retention not only as a profit generator but as providing a contribution to profits much greater than the old business gods of market share, cost reduction or new products. Yet, although companies mouth customer retention as a strategy for improving financial performance, practice lags woefully behind the rhetoric.

Corporate Myopia on Customer Retention

The REL Consultancy Group conducted a survey on customer retention and corporate profitability and explored specific business practices influencing retention among Fortune 500 companies.[8] It found some startling results, reflecting the tunnel vision of senior corporate executives regarding customer retention and loyalty.

THE CUSTOMER LOYALTY AUDIT

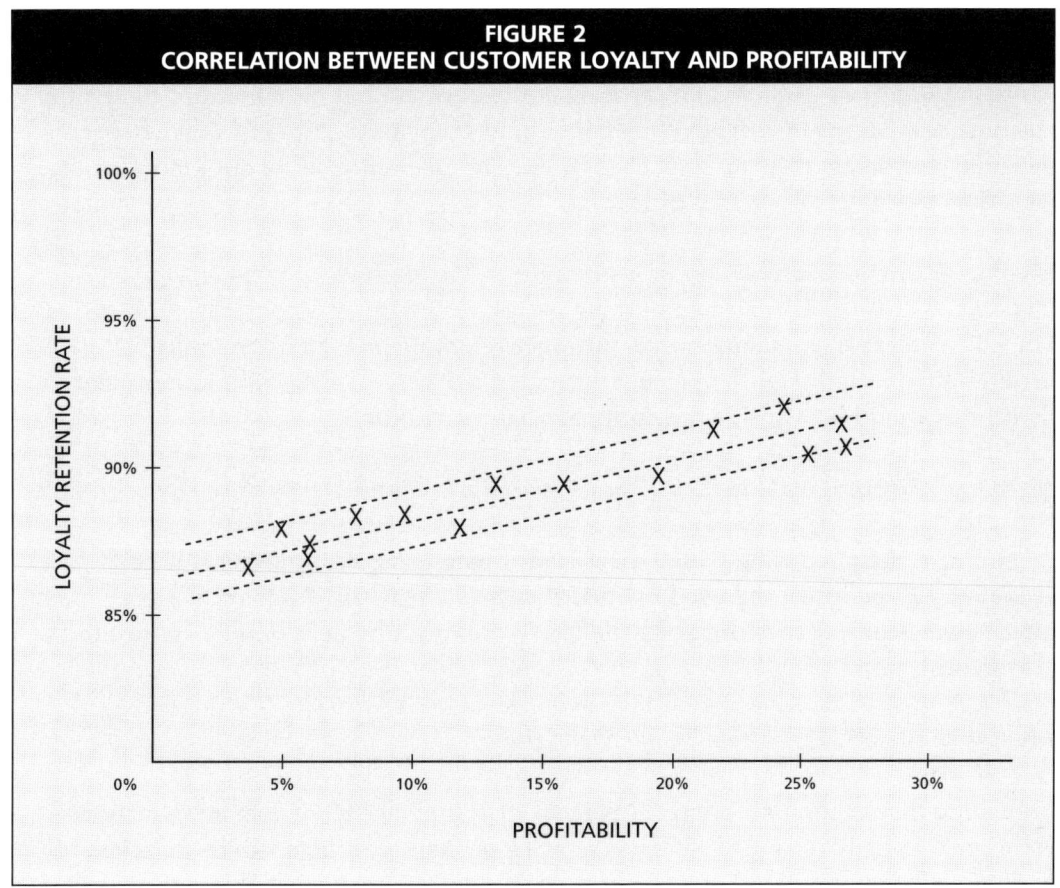

Myopia 1: Defection Rates

Half the survey participants reported a defection rate of at least 10 percent. One out of four reported a defection rate of at least 20 percent and one out of ten a defection rate of at least 30 percent. Other surveys estimate a much higher average defection rate of 25 percent. Any company exceeding a maximum defection rate of 10 percent is headed for serious trouble.

Myopia 2: Customer Defection Impact on Sales

An unbelievable 61 percent of survey participants felt customer defections had an insignificant impact on sales. Worse, one in seven felt customer defections would have no impact on sales!

Myopia 3: Action on Defecting Customers

More than one out of three participating companies did not even attempt to identify customers in danger of leaving. One out of four companies did not bother to ask defecting customers their reasons for leaving; and one out of three took no action regarding customers in danger of leaving.

Myopia 4: Customer Retention as a Measure of Profitability

Only 17 percent of companies used customer retention as a metric to improve profitability (even though 69 percent estimated a 5 percent reduction in customer defections would have a significant impact on profitability).

Myopia 5: Fixation on Cost Reduction, New Markets and Developing New Products

By contrast, the most widely used measure for increasing profitability was cost reduction (23 percent), followed by identifying new markets (18 percent) — i.e. going after new customers and forgetting the old — followed by developing new products (18 percent).

Myopia 6: Main Cause of Customer Defections

Extending this fixation on price, 27 percent of companies felt customer defections were predominantly price related and only 16 percent saw them as service related (in reality, as shown in Table 1, service was given a rating by the customers themselves of 65 points out of 100 as the ideal characteristic of a supplier).

Balancing these uniformed perceptions, however, the REL survey did register a few positive and encouraging trends:

Impact on Profits by Reducing Customer Defections

81 percent of participants felt there would be a profit increase if they addressed the avoidable reasons for customer defections — 43 percent estimated a 1 to 5 percent profit increase; 25 percent a 5 to 10 percent profit increase and 12 percent felt there would be more than a 10 percent increase in profits. Heartening as these perceptions are, the profit potential of retaining customers is estimated by experts as being much higher — at a whopping 50 percent increase!

Understanding of Relationship Between Customer Defection Rates and Profitability

76 percent of companies understood the tie-in between customer defection rates and profitability — 23 percent specifically and quantitatively, while 53 percent understood it intuitively but not specifically.

Customer Retention Given a Higher Priority in the Next Five Years

78 percent of participants expected customer retention to become a higher priority in the next five years.

Customer Loyalty a Target in Sales and Marketing Programs

92 percent of participants felt maintaining customer loyalty was a factor in targeting sales and marketing programs — with 40 percent agreeing specifically and quantitatively and the other 52 percent agreeing intuitively but not specifically.

CUSTOMER DIFFERENTIATION: FOCUS ON "CORE" CUSTOMERS

Management guru Peter Drucker claims companies cannot afford to be in too many businesses at the same time. They must make a concentrated decision and focus on businesses in which they excel. Peters and Waterman, in their book *In Search of Excellence*,[9] emphasize the same concept when they state companies "should stick to their knitting," i.e. concentrate on those businesses in which they are most competent.

Customer Portfolio Analysis

Modeled after the well-known BCG portfolio analysis for business concentration, this author has developed a similar chart for differentiating between types of customers, each requiring a different corporate strategy to deal with them.[10] Figure 3 shows two axes — corporate profitability and added value to the customer — the two fundamental objectives of any corporation. The two axes create four customer categories:

1. "Dog" Customers

Referring to customers as dogs is in poor taste. But several kinds of customers are really not worth keeping. An article on "Customer Satisfaction Fables"[11] states: "The briefest inquiry to any sales force will confirm that some customers are uninformed, unrealistic and demanding. Most businesses have certain segments of customers who are not profitably worth satisfying."

Even if customers are not hostile, at least 20 percent of the total customer population is not profitable to a company for a variety of reasons — low volume, incompatibility, a tendency to drive the price down to the exclusion of any other perceived value. Such customers are candidates for termination, through price increases or other means.

2. Satisfied Customers

This group of customers should always receive — and perceive — a high level of satisfaction, but should not divert a company's concentration on its "core" customers (Category 4). Satisfied customers constitute 40–50 percent of the total customer population. They include both industrial customers and public end users, large in number but small in sales. They do not expect a large increase in their perceived

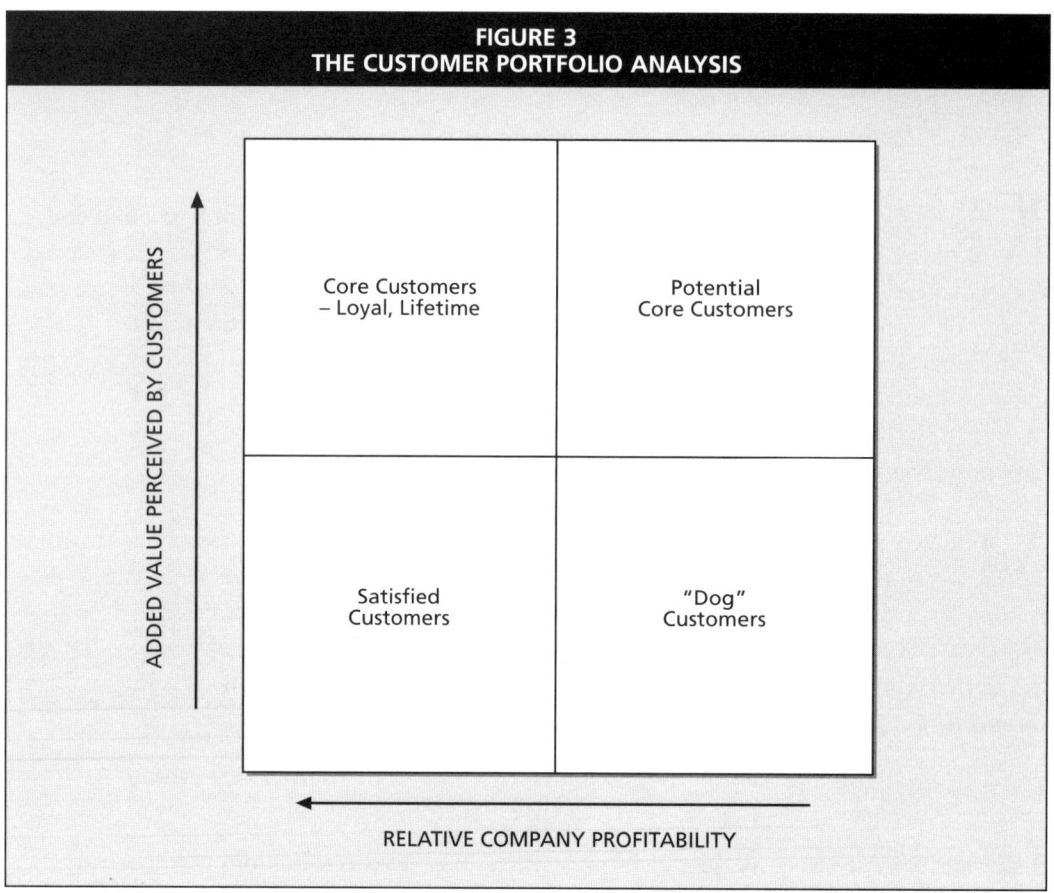

added value as a result of purchases from a supplier. The company also does not derive much profit from this group.

3. Potential "Core" Customers

This group of customers may not be profitable in the short term, but they have the potential to become core customers in the long run, with perceived added value to themselves and a resultant high profit to the company. They need to be cultivated.

4. Star "Core" Customers

Following the Pareto principle, this core group of customers constitutes 20 percent or fewer of all customers but accounts for 80 percent or more of the company's sales volume and its profits. A company best serves this group by what it adds to its customers' value. It uses its expertise and application skills in technology, quality, cost, cycle time, people empowerment, etc. to help its customer companies become more competitive and more profitable in one or more of the above areas. The added value its customers perceive must be continuously nurtured so they become customers for life. This briefing concentrates on this core group of customers.

Internal Customers

There is a level of customer different from the categories cited above: the internal customer. Companies respect their external customers, especially the core customers. But the internal customer — the next operation to receive the work of a previous process, be it a business process, a design process or a manufacturing process — is often treated like dirt. There is little love lost between an internal customer and an internal supplier in the interminable turf wars between departments. As an example, manufacturing is engineering's most important internal customer. Yet engineering often considers manufacturing to be a second-class citizen, tossing a product half-baked over the wall — with the time-bomb ticking — for manufacturing to catch and muddle through.

In the new age of customer satisfaction and loyalty, the internal customer must be elevated to a high status — if not to a king, as is the external customer, then at least to a prince. Every process, be it a product or service, has an internal customer whose requirements must be assessed, similar to those of the external customer. Internal customer feedback and measurements should similarly be sought. And those evaluations should be more important than performance appraisals by the boss. In progressive companies, internal customer appraisals are replacing boss appraisals to determine merit increases and promotions.[12] Sometimes, the internal customer can terminate the internal supplier because of continued poor performance; and in extreme cases even go outside the company for service.

Peripheral Customers

In addition to external and internal customers, a company has other peripheral customers who cannot be neglected:

Former customers

These "dropouts" must be identified. Their reasons for leaving the company must be scrutinized and a concerted effort made to win them back, especially if they are in the core group.

Non-customers

Many companies neglect this key group. Attempting to analyze why non-customers stay away from a company can go a long way in enticing them. Some of the more common reasons are lack of knowledge of the company or its products; lack of advertising; price; poor public image (unfavorable media publicity); dissatisfaction with one element in a supply chain (e.g. not choosing a manufacturer because of an unfavorable experience with a distributor); or because of bad comments by friends and relatives.

Other stakeholders

A company has several stakeholders in addition to customers. Suppliers, distributors, dealers and stockholders are, in a broader sense, customers who should be served. Stakeholders are sometimes taken for granted. Universities and other educational institutions pay scant attention to students as customers, for example. They pay even less attention to the industry hiring their "product" or to parents paying them. In hospitals, doctors do not look on their patients as customers, nor do their administrators and other support staff.

The public

Finally, a company has an obligation to serve not only its stakeholders, including customers, but the public as well. Since a company derives its ultimate legitimacy from the community and the country in which it operates, its customers-at-large are the public. Public perceptions of a company as a corporate citizen — in terms of integrity, employment, non-discrimination, environmental and social responsibility — are important attributes of its character, its citizenship and its usefulness to society. If a company loses its public image, its public trust, it deserves to go out of business.

The Ten Inviolate Principles of Customer Loyalty

Principles have governed relationships among people, societies, religions and countries for over 5000 years. They represent an anchor of faith and stability in a changing and uncertain world. They provide a moral compass.

It is essential, therefore, for customer loyalty and retention to be governed by a set of unchanging, steadfast principles to cement a long-term marriage between a company and its core customers.

Principle 1: Added Value in a Customer–Supplier Partnership

It is fashionable to speak of a win–win partnership between a company and its customers and between a company and its suppliers. But most companies claiming such partnerships have not advanced them much beyond the slogan stage. The emphasis is still on "what's in it for me." The first principle, therefore, must be for a company to firmly believe it exists to add true value to its customers. The added value must be perceived by the customer in the form of improving its quality, cost, cycle time, technology and people empowerment — all leading to greater competitiveness and profit for the customer. Obviously, the reward for added customer value is a loyal customer who contributes higher profits to the supplier company on a sustained long-term basis. Profit is a result, not a cause; an output, not an input.

By the same token, the reciprocal principle of the core customer should be to establish a firm partnership with key suppliers and help them with quality, cost, cycle time and profit improvement, as the best and surest way to help itself.

Principle 2: A Partnership Based on Ethics and Uncompromising Integrity

Corporate ethics seem as rare as individual ethics. Companies are regularly cited for financial skullduggery, environmental violations, bribes, kickbacks and other violations. These firms may win out in the short run but lose their corporate souls and even their very existence in the long run. A corporation with uncompromising integrity is not only successful over time, but is held up for other companies to emulate as a role model.

At Motorola many years ago, a very lucrative contract for a multimillion-dollar communications system with a Latin American government seemed to be in the bag, when its high-ranking procurement official asked for a kickback. Even though this was considered the norm for doing business with this country, Bob Galvin, the chairman of the board, issued a flat and firm edict that the company would rather lose business than be a party to unethical practices anywhere in the world.[13] Today, the Motorola folklore is filled with anecdotes about Galvin's uncompromising integrity and how he has promoted ethics as a top corporate value. Motorola's success as one of the best-managed companies in the world is a tribute to the long-range economic value of ethics. A high-ranking official in China categorically stated the Chinese government would prefer to do business with Motorola every time because of its well-earned reputation for scrupulous honesty.

Principle 3: Mutual Trust: the Self-Fulfilling Prophecy

When a teacher looks on students as stupid and incorrigible, they respond by fulfilling the teacher's lowest expectations. On the other hand, when a teacher has faith in the students, trusts them and encourages them to reach for their best potential, the students rise to the challenge of the self-fulfilling prophecy.

Similarly, managers who do not trust their employees and have little faith in their ability or effort are met with sullen employees attesting to the managers' low expectations. The employees' trust in the managers is equally low. True leaders trust their people, have faith in their creativity and encourage them to grow to their full potential. Trust is a logical outgrowth of principles and ethics. It takes time to build but it is enduring in terms of the loyalty it engenders on both sides.

Principle 4: Sharing Technology, Strategy and Cost Data

The "open kimono" policy — a term first used at Xerox — is the epitome of trust. It means a company is willing to open its books on its technology, its corporate strategies and its cost data to its core customers and the latter are willing to do the same. Very few companies have graduated to this level of trust and openness, but it is the essence of true partnership. For all practical purposes, the company is an extension of the core customer, except for ownership and finance.

Principle 5: Mutual, Active, Concrete Help

A distinct feature of the vital difference between the fewer than 10 percent of successful partnerships between companies and their customers and the more than 90 percent of partnerships-in-name-only is the amount of active, concrete help rendered between customer and supplier companies.

In the quality arena, as an example, supplier certification is seen as a silver bullet for outstanding quality success. Customer companies audit their key suppliers once or twice a year and expect the latter to achieve very high levels of quality as a result. The great majority of such certified suppliers barely register even a 50 percent improvement. For customer companies to effect a tenfold and even a hundredfold supplier quality improvement in one or two years — levels desperately needed for industry to be globally competitive — they must visit and help their partnership suppliers frequently, at least once a week until substantial improvements are under way.

They must coach the suppliers in powerful tools for quality improvement[14] such as the design of experiments, multiple environment over stress tests, quality function deployment, poka yoke and the costs of poor quality. They must coach suppliers in tools for cost improvement, such as value engineering, group technology and learning/experience curves. They must coach suppliers in tools for cycle time reduction, such as total productive maintenance, focus factories, pull vs. push systems, small lots with very short changeover time, and process flows. There may also be other coaching on management, organizational development, design, manufacturing, people empowerment, etc. Such coaching entails not just classroom training but also hands-on help. Yet fewer than 1 percent of a customer's so-called professionals are equipped to render such in-depth coaching.

On the supplier's side, there must be reciprocal active, concrete help. This includes early supplier involvement in design, value engineering ideas, cost targeting, and determining meaningful but mutually acceptable specifications — in short, all areas where the supplier's expertise is greater than the customer's and which can lead to greater customer productivity, competitiveness and profit.

Frequently asked questions include: Why should a customer company spend valuable time and human resources on coaching partnership suppliers? And why should suppliers spend their time and resources rendering concrete help to partnership customers? The answer to the first question is it is the best way for a customer to help itself to achieve significant improvement in quality, cost and cycle time. The answer to the second is it is the best way for the customer to perceive the supplier's added value to the customer and greater profit for itself. Further, such reciprocal help is the essence of goodwill, partnership and loyalty.

Principle 6: Action on All Elements of Customer Enthusiasm

Figure 4 represents a network of 20 elements combining to produce customer enthusiasm for products. This is a formidable list of the factors influencing a customer — which of these elements is the most important? The engineer would say "technical performance," the salesforce would opt for "features," the quality professionals would select "quality" and so on. The answer is no one element is more important than others at all times, in all places, for all customers. In varying degrees, however, they all add up to customer enthusiasm, customer delight, customer value.

The Customer Loyalty Audit

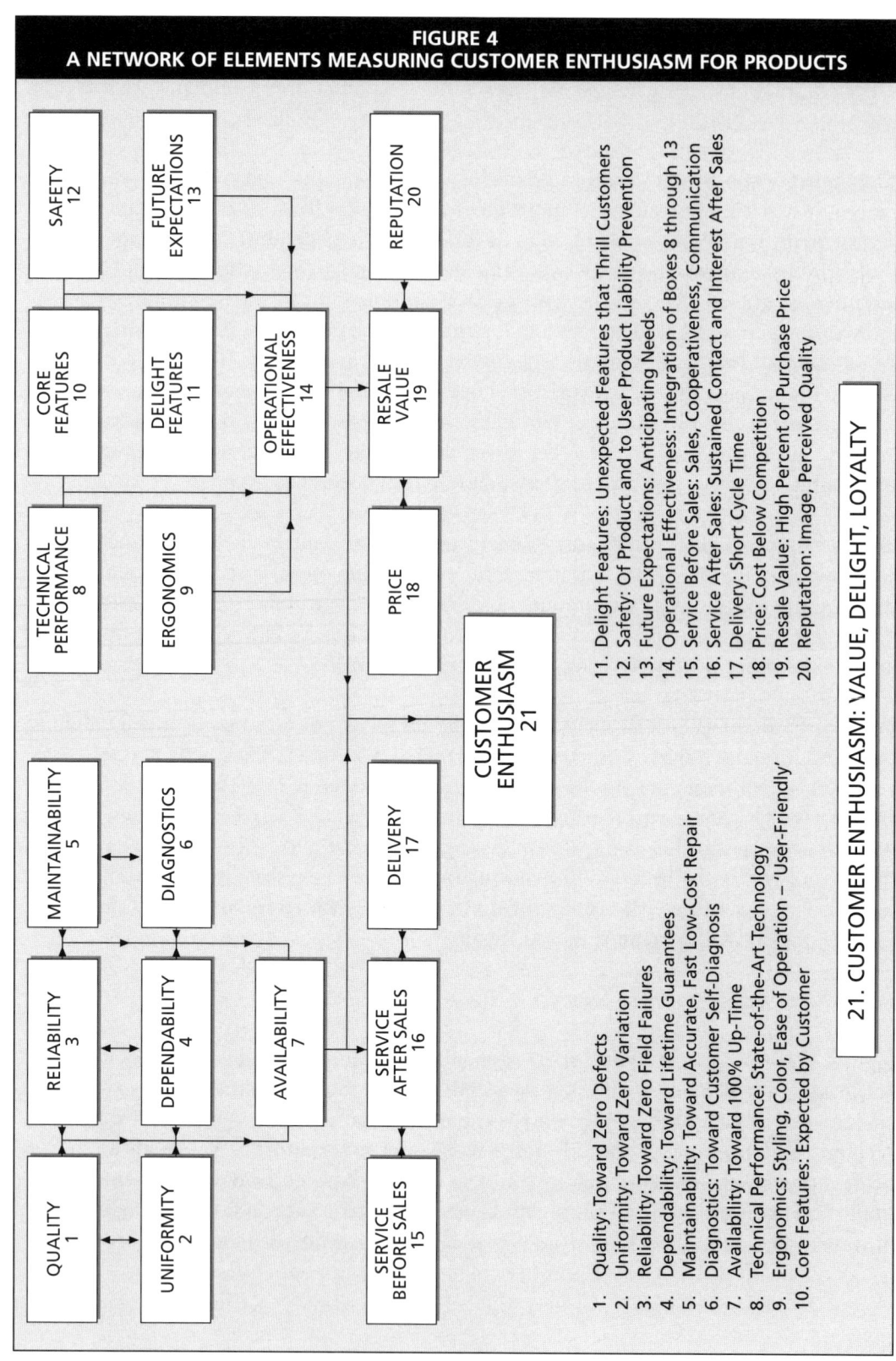

This author has developed a theory on customer enthusiasm, dubbed "Bhote's Law" by his college students. This states:

1. The most important elements of customer enthusiasm are those elements the customer stresses as important. If these are missing from a product, they merit top management's urgent action.

2. The best way to determine what customers deem important is to ask them, through quality function deployment and other techniques, detailed in Step 3. For the core customer, this determination must be even more detailed, on a one-on-one basis.[15]

For example, American cars had dominated the US car market with a larger than 90 percent share until the early 1970s. But the public was disgusted with the quality of US-made cars. The Japanese saw quality as their market niche and boldly invaded US car makers' turf to capture up to 30 percent of the market. (Were it not for voluntary restrictions on their part, the figure could have risen to 50 percent.) Belatedly, the US car makers moved to reduce the quality gap and, based on the J.D. Powers ratings, are recapturing at least 30 percent of the market share lost to the Japanese.

Figure 5 shows a similar network of elements combining to produce customer enthusiasm in the service industry. The elements are somewhat different from those associated with products, but the approach is the same and Bhote's Law applies to services with equal validity.

Principle 7: Focus on the Unexpected to Generate Customer Delight

In the battle for features, most companies do provide a core of features which the customer expects and gets. Quality, sometimes mistakenly equated with features, is also in the same league. The rising expectations of the car buyer, for example, have reduced features and quality to a given. They prevent customers from defecting but they no longer excite them. The latest trend is to develop some feature which customers do not know about or anticipate, but which excites them when included. Here again, Japanese car makers have stolen a march. For the last three years, Japanese car owners have had an electronic map locator to tell them where they are and the best route to a particular destination. This is only now being talked about as a feature among the US Big Three.

In the service industry, the Sheraton Towers Hotel in Singapore is an excellent example of how offering the unexpected generates customer delight and subsequent loyalty. When you enter the lobby, the bellman does not take you to the registration desk but directly to an assistant manager who, surprisingly, already knows your name. With no waiting in line, you are ushered to your room. Moments later, a "butler" comes in to check if everything is to your satisfaction. He or she offers to press your suits and shine your shoes free of charge. A maid brings in a whole

The Customer Loyalty Audit

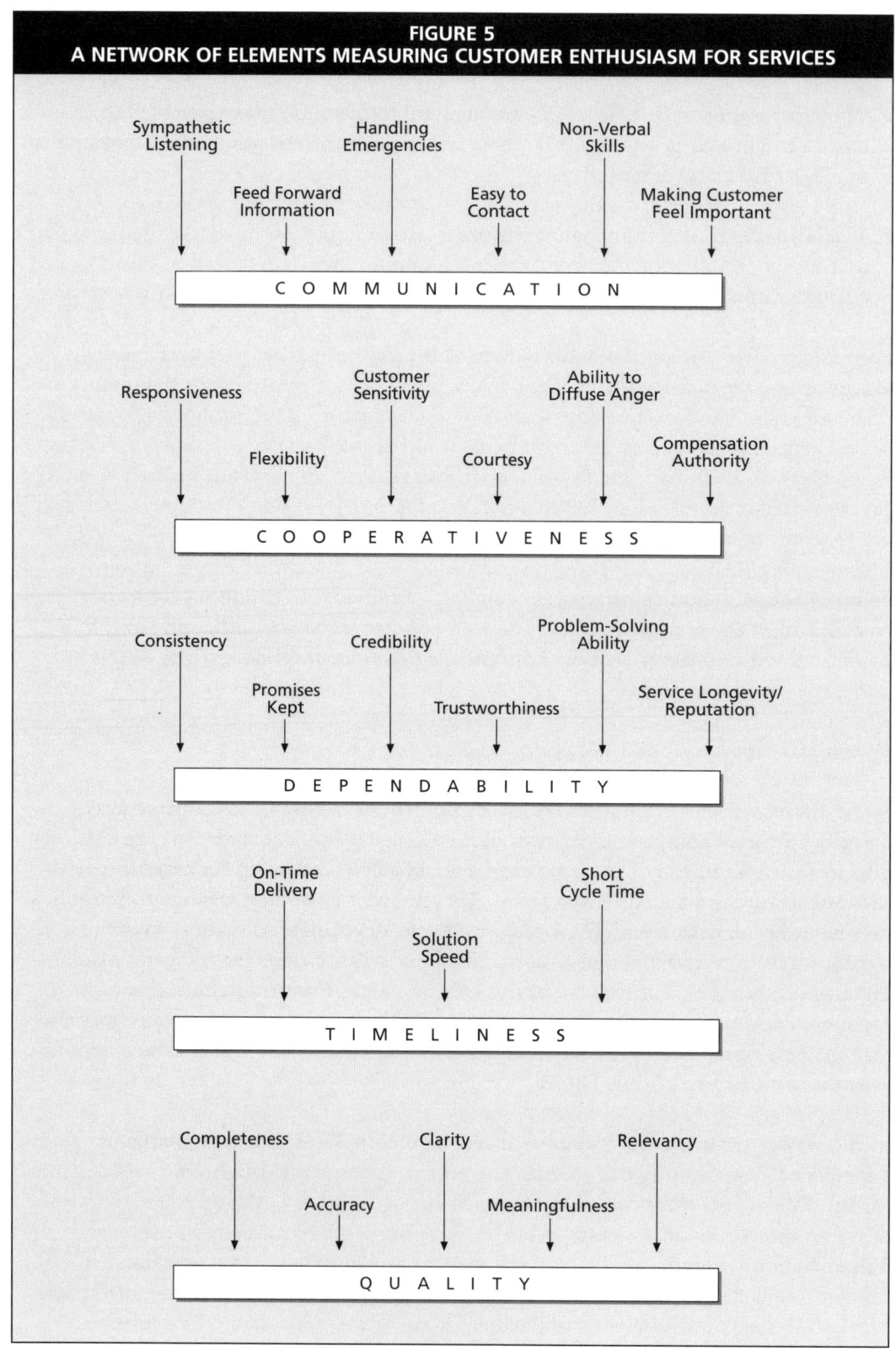

FIGURE 5: A NETWORK OF ELEMENTS MEASURING CUSTOMER ENTHUSIASM FOR SERVICES

complimentary case of toiletries. In the afternoon, a snack is served with your tea. The general manager asks you to join him in the evening for free cocktails and hors d'oeuvres. The evening ends with a rich dessert served in your room before bedtime. Wakeup calls come with free tea or coffee and the morning newspaper of your choice. The staff on your floor greet you by name. This is the difference between mere customer satisfaction and customer delight. The payoff is the customer returning to the same hotel, despite the existence of more luxurious but "cold" hotels without the personal touch.

Principle 8: Closeness to the Customer

Konusuke Matsushita, the legendary founder of the Matsushita electronics empire, would counsel his salesforce to "take the customer's skin temperature every day." Bonds of trust between a company and its core customers are largely based on close, personal relationships between individuals in the two companies. This is not just friendship or favoritism, it is confidence that each person is working to help the partner company for mutual benefit.

A survey for AT&T examined the factors involved in sales wins versus sales losses. These included the complexity of equipment; size of orders; comparisons with competition; characteristics of the account executive; the ratio of the number of account executives to the technical advisers, etc. The results, using a paired comparison technique, revealed the greatest correlation to success was the amount of time spent with the customer and the ensuing personal relationship of mutual respect and trust.

Another perspective on closeness to the customer is top management personally spending time with its core customers. A 1988 survey by Learning Dynamics[16] shows 40 percent of senior managers spending less than 10 percent of their time with customers and 34 percent spending more than a quarter of their time with customers — what a bipolar distribution! Top management often loves to sit in its ivory tower, issuing mission statements and policies. While these are important, they are no substitute for getting out into the real world of customers, where the action is.

Motorola's Bob Galvin again set the trend in 1986 when he personally selected and visited his top ten customers. He did not meet with his counterpart CEOs but with the employees who actually used Motorola's products. He spent a whole day with each customer and got unfiltered feedback. The visits were so rewarding he institutionalized this procedure, requiring every senior executive to visit ten of their top customers each year.

A similar effort, not only for core customers but also for individual end users on a random basis, holds great promise for customer loyalty. One vice-president of a large television company would select two households owning his firm's TV sets to visit each time he went out of town for business meetings. The impact on the home owners was electrifying. "Can you imagine," they would excitedly tell their friends and neighbors, "a top VP of a multinational firm actually spent an hour of his valuable time with us, sincerely listening to our comments — good and bad — and taking action!" This word-of-mouth communication proved to be more powerful in these communities than any advertisement.

From an organizational perspective, closeness to the customer requires a member of the company's top management to be formally appointed as the customer's advocate within the firm. A senior executive as ombudsman, i.e. a troubleshooter for customer complaints, is not good enough. If a company can have a COO (Chief Operating Officer) and a CFO (Chief Financial Officer), the least it can do is create a CCO (Chief Customer Officer) who would rank second in importance after the CEO (Chief Executive Officer). Yet, according to the Learning Dynamics' survey, only 7 percent of companies reported having a CCO. In 41 percent of companies, salespeople are the only ones representing the customer's point of view. In another 38 percent, the customer service representative is the lone voice of the customer.

Finally, from a human resources perspective, closeness to the customer must equate to closeness to employees. Employees, especially the frontline troops who come into frequent contact with customers, must have sufficient administrative, managerial and financial freedom to deal with customers on the spot and to back them up on their decisions, even if it means added expense to the company. In a larger sense, it means giving employees not just token empowerment, as most companies seem to do, but real empowerment, as perceived by the employees themselves.

Principle 9: Genuine Interest in the Customer After the Sale Is Consummated

A survey of why car buyers did not develop loyalty to their dealers and return to them for their next purchase revealed the great majority — 68 percent — felt "the dealer didn't give a damn." The morale here is loyalty is assured by never forgetting the customer, even long after the sale has been consummated. Service is said to be five times as important to the customer as price and close attention to the customer after sale is five times as important as service, in terms of long-term loyalty.

One car salesman who won a national reputation for selling twice as many cars as the second-best salesperson calls his customers soon after the sale and periodically thereafter to solicit their reactions and help them. He calls them on their birthdays, alerts them to their next service checkup, helps them resolve any servicing problems and even assists in the resale of their cars.

Enterprising grocery stores keep track of their regular customers, the frequency of their visits, the amounts they buy, their product selections, their favorite brands, etc. They inform these loyal customers of special items about to go on sale, send out discount coupons and above all get to know and greet them as friends. (Of course, this would not have been possible in the pre-computer, pre-information technology age.) All of this costs time and money in a business with the slenderest of profit margins. But the return on investment in a typical loyal customer who spends $3000 to $6000 a year at the store is worth going the extra mile. Similar methodologies are coming into vogue at banks, insurance companies, hotels, airlines and other services to add value for their loyal customers.

Principle 10: Anticipation of Future Customer Needs and Expectations

It is one thing to determine the current needs of existing customers, but it is quite another to peek into the future and anticipate the changing needs of current customers, their unmet and even unknown future expectations. Fortunately, there are techniques a company can use to polish its crystal ball. It can:

- Involve top management with the core customer's top management in business, market and product strategy.

- Institute a joint customer–supplier product or service planning process.

- Start joint R&D projects with key engineering and marketing personnel from the customer company.

- Organize round tables, focus groups and clinics using a small sample of the public likely to be the "center of gravity" of the target market.

- Benchmark best-in-class companies with an established track record of anticipating customer needs and expectations.

Some critics believe there is not much use in sharing a company's innovations and working with customers who may be totally unaware of such innovations or their practical applications. But major innovations and technical breakthroughs are not an everyday occurrence, they occur only once or twice per decade. Going from vacuum tubes to transistors, from transistors to integrated circuits and microprocessors and from mobile radios to cellular phones are examples of such breakthroughs. In the meantime, hundreds of opportunities for new products and services are occurring all the time, in a steady stream of smaller innovations where the customer's involvement is not only desirable but should be eagerly sought. This makes the difference between an occasional home run and a hit every time at bat.

It is well known that 80 percent of all new products in the marketplace are the result of customer ideas and suggestions. Consider for instance the service of a concierge in a hotel. For years, such services were confined to routine matters: road directions, airline confirmations, theater tickets. But customers have been expanding the horizons of a concierge, from hotels to office buildings, and from routine services to meals, flowers, laundry and many more services the harried office executive is only too happy to pay for.

Part 2

A Seven-Step Audit for Attaining and Maintaining Customer Loyalty

Step 1

TOP MANAGEMENT COMMITMENT AND INVOLVEMENT

Jay Sprechler, in his book *When America Does It Right*, examines customer services of the 56 companies named the most admired by *Fortune* magazine. He states: "Without the CEO's attention, customer service can be neglected and wither away… There isn't a single case where customer service developed from a bottom-up approach… The CEO can never walk away from maintaining a direct, highly visible and pervasive involvement."

The difference between words and deeds, between mere top management support and its involvement, is illustrated by the old story of the hen and the pig who wanted to reward the farmer for having taken such good care of them. They decided to make breakfast. The hen brightly suggested ham and eggs. The pig protested. "Oh no," he said, "yours is support, mine is involvement." Top management must "walk the talk."

Values — Not a NATO Game

Walking the talk extends to corporate values as well. Many CEOs spend a considerable amount of time formulating values or beliefs for their corporations. These values are a "magnetic north," a compass to guide the activities of all employees. But a number of CEOs stop after publishing these values. They become a "NATO" (No Action, Talk Only) exercise, a wall-hanging. For values to have true value, they must be lived and breathed by top management, disseminated to all employees, studied by them and — most importantly — accepted by them.

A good way to gain employee acceptance is for top managers to model the behavior they want. Behavioral scientists claim behaviors are learnt from past experiences where such behavior has been rewarded or ignored or punished. A behavior followed by a reward is a positive reinforcement and likely to be repeated, while a behavior followed by punishment is a strong deterrent and not likely to be repeated.

Demonstrating Customer Commitment to Employees

Employees use a number of symbols to gauge whether top management truly pursues customer satisfaction and loyalty:

- Attention to the metrics associated with customer satisfaction and especially customer loyalty (see Step 5).

- Uncompromising integrity in dealing with customers and the public.

THE CUSTOMER LOYALTY AUDIT

- Trust in employees and their ability to grow as a reflection of trust in customers.

- Strong and urgent corrective action on the element of customer satisfaction missing from the company's product.

- Personally spending time with customers.

- Committing resources: time, personal attention and money.

- Giving customer-contact employees authorization to make their own decisions in dealing with customers — especially irate ones — even if it costs the company to do so.

- Rewarding those employees who provide excellent customer service and celebrating such achievers.

- Communicating the commitment to the customer in publications, advertisements, newsletters, news releases to the media and annual reports.

- Encouraging feedback from employees, publicising and rewarding their ideas.

- Establishing customer satisfaction and loyalty as a key part of the agenda at periodic meetings.

Customer Loyalty Audit and Scoring System

Each step of the process for attaining and retaining customer loyalty contains a self-assessment audit to measure its effectiveness. This is best done by a cross-functional team, consisting of a member from top management, preferably the Chief Customer Officer (CCO), sales/marketing, service, quality assurance and, especially, a representative from customer-contact employees.

Rating

The audit lists several success factors contributing to the effectiveness of each step. Each success factor should be given a rating of 1 to 5 by the self-assessment team, with 1 being the worst and 5 being the best, using the following criteria:

THE CUSTOMER LOYALTY AUDIT

Rating	Criteria
1	No knowledge of the success factor
2	Only a conceptual awareness of the success factor
3	Success factor started, with less than 50 percent implementation
4	Success factor 50 to 80 percent implemented
5	Success factor implementation over 80 percent, along with reflected improvements in customer loyalty metrics and business results.

TOP MANAGEMENT COMMITMENT AND INVOLVEMENT AUDIT

		RATING 1 2 3 4 5
A.	**Inviolate Principles of Customer Loyalty (Core Customers)**	
1.	Perceived added value. The company's core customers perceive it has added value to their own operations – in terms of improved quality, cost, cycle time, innovations, technology etc. – all leading to their greater competitiveness and profitability.	
2.	The company is perceived by its core customers and the public as having uncompromising ethics.	
3.	There is a climate of mutual trust between the company and its core customers that fuels a win–win partnership.	
4.	There is an "open kimono" policy between the company and its core customers – a complete sharing of each other's technology, strategy and cost data.	
5.	The company renders active help to its core customers, including early involvement in design, value engineering ideas and cost targeting.	
6.	The company focuses on that element of customer satisfaction that is important to the customer and missing from its products or services.	
7.	The company focuses on product or service innovations that customers do not expect but delight them when introduced.	
8.	Closeness to the customer is assured through developing close personal relationships and appointing a Chief Customer Officer (CCO) as the customer's advocate.	
9.	The company displays genuine interest in the customer long after the sale is consummated.	
10.	The company anticipates the customer's future and changing needs with joint R&D projects, focus groups and clinics.	

		RATING 1 2 3 4 5
B.	**Management "Walking The Talk"**	
1.	Top management spends a minimum of 25% of its personal time dealing with its core customers.	
2.	It visits its core customers at least once a year, spending time with the actual users of its products and services.	
3.	It assures that its senior executives visit their key customers, receiving feedback and suggestions from them.	
4.	It visits its customer-contact personnel, its field offices and its service centers a minimum of once per year for multinational companies and several times a year for smaller companies.	
5.	It conducts Management by Wandering Around (MBWA) among all its employees, listening to them, encouraging and supporting them and acting on their ideas.	
6.	It conducts rap sessions with small groups of employees to listen to their concerns, remove roadblocks in their path and permit them to focus on the customer.	
7.	It not only shuts down a product line when quality or other characteristics adversely affects a customer, but encourages and authorizes all employees to do so if customer satisfaction is jeopardized.	
C.	**Behavior Reinforcement**	
1.	Top management reinforces adherence to customer satisfaction with recognition and awards to employees enhancing customer loyalty.	
2.	Top management deters employee neglect or indifference to customers with appropriate disincentives.	
D.	**Demonstrating Commitment to Employees**	
1.	Top management has developed, implemented and monitored a system of metrics to gauge customer satisfaction and loyalty.	
2.	It supports its employees with resources, time and personal attention to focus their energies on customer satisfaction.	
3.	It emphasizes those company policies and procedures directly affecting the customer and de-emphasizes (or even eliminates) those of no consequence to the customer.	
4.	It authorizes contact employees to use their own discretion in dealing with customers, including financial compensation within guidelines.	
5.	It encourages innovative ideas from employees in addressing customer issues publicizing and rewarding such ideas.	
6.	It recognizes and rewards those employees who provide excellent customer service and celebrates their achievements throughout the company.	
7.	It communicates its commitment to the customer in all its publications: newsletters, videotapes, bulletins, quarterly and annual reports.	
8.	It establishes customer satisfaction and loyalty as a key agenda item at its periodic review meetings, even elevating the item to the first place in the agenda.	

Step 2

INTERNAL BENCHMARKING — ESTABLISHING A BASELINE

Once a company decides customer loyalty is its most important objective and its top management has made an unequivocal commitment to pursue the objective, it must determine its current status — where it is positioned on the road to customer loyalty.

This step will help a company conduct an internal benchmarking study and establish a baseline for further improvement. It is divided into the main categories of a company's activities, starting with measurement and assessing its people, management, organization, systems, tools, design, suppliers, manufacturing, field and support services.

Measurement

What the benchmarking measures includes the following:

Customer Loyalty

The number and percentage of loyal customers and their longevity are assessed.

Value Added to Core Customers

This indicates money saved for core customers, as measured by them.

Cost of Poor Quality

Although mainly used as a total quality management (TQM) metric, the cost of poor quality integrates the failings of management, human resources, products and services. Figure 6 depicts several elements associated with the cost of poor quality. Like an iceberg, where only the top shows and the greater portion is submerged in the ocean, a mere 20 percent of the costs of poor quality are traditionally picked up by the accounting department. Even this small percentage amounts to between 5 and 10 percent of sales — a huge waste. For some companies, the cost of poor quality is an amazing $100 to $200 per employee, per day.

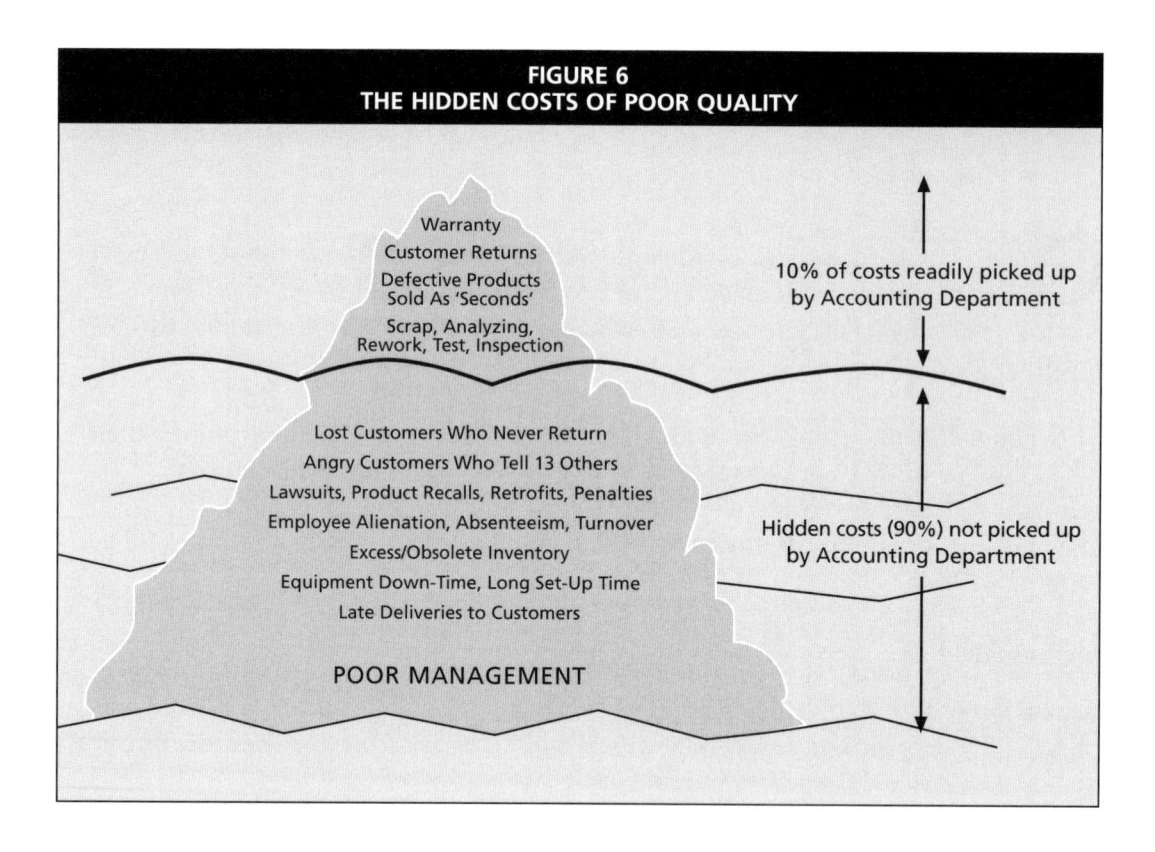

FIGURE 6
THE HIDDEN COSTS OF POOR QUALITY

Warranty
Customer Returns
Defective Products Sold As 'Seconds'
Scrap, Analyzing, Rework, Test, Inspection

10% of costs readily picked up by Accounting Department

Lost Customers Who Never Return
Angry Customers Who Tell 13 Others
Lawsuits, Product Recalls, Retrofits, Penalties
Employee Alienation, Absenteeism, Turnover
Excess/Obsolete Inventory
Equipment Down-Time, Long Set-Up Time
Late Deliveries to Customers

POOR MANAGEMENT

Hidden costs (90%) not picked up by Accounting Department

But the more insidious costs are those conventional accounting has not been able to gather. Amounting to 80 percent of the costs of poor quality, they can account for a whopping 20 to 40 percent of sales.

Let's take just one element among these hidden costs of poor quality, lost customers.

Probable cost	=	Average sales to a customer per year
	x	number of customers lost per year (the average 25% of the customer base)
	x	the average number of longer-term lost purchases
	+	the potential loss of sales from an average of nine friends of each lost customer

For a car dealership, with an average sale of, say, $20,000, with a loss of just 10 customers per year and a loss of repeat business 10 times over a buyer's adult lifetime, the defection loss adds up to a staggering $2 million, not counting the potential turning away of friends and neighbors.

And what about the cost of poor quality/poor customer loyalty traceable to poor management? It is estimated the very best CEOs make the right decisions about 70 percent of the time, with the average CEO falling below the 50 percent mark. What is the cost of these poor decisions in terms of customers, resources, structure, systems and people?

Between these two elements alone — lost customers and poor management — it is a wonder many companies are still in business.

Cycle Time

Cycle time is the other half of the quality coin. It can be defined as the clock time from the start of a process — either a manufacturing, business, design or service process — to its completion. The direct labor time for the process — known as theoretical cycle time — is only a small fraction (less than 10 percent) of this total cycle time. The rest is *waste* — waiting time, set-up time, transport time, storage time, inspection and test time, rework time and approval time.

It is important to assess the current cycle time for customer orders, new product introduction, manufacturing and key business processes such as accounts receivable and accounts payable.

People

This is a significant assessment category. In the final analysis, service is a relationship between employees and customers. If a company devalues its employees, employees will pass this message on to customers. People cannot be treated merely as a pair of hands. They cannot give of their best in a climate of fear, of lack of trust. They must be listened to, supported, encouraged, trained and given opportunities to grow to their full potential. And true empowerment means giving them a piece of the action, administrative, managerial and financial.

Management

Step 1 detailed the salient features of a top management baseline: commitment and involvement, "walking the talk," superordinate values, rewarding behaviors reinforcing customer service, and demonstrating customer commitment by thought, word and deed.

Organization

In the best tradition of business process reengineering, a company should evaluate whether it is moving away from bureaucracy, with its organizational charts and neat little boxes of departments, towards cross-functional teams, such as customer development, new product development, customer order etc. It should also assess whether the internal customer has been elevated to a position of importance, as scorekeeper and evaluator of the internal supplier's performance.

System

The assessment in this category should focus on whether policies and procedures exist for the good of the customer or for command and control by management. It should also examine whether the old practices in hiring, training, evaluations, merit raises and promotions have been revolutionized to change the behavior and values of employees and move to a customer-focused culture.

Tools

Tools have, traditionally, been a weak link in most companies and in many disciplines. Tools of the trade in determining customer requirements and satisfying them — such as market research, mail surveys, a fixation on features (leading to feature "creep"), technological breakthroughs, and an overemphasis on quality for the sake of quality alone — are weak techniques. They dilute concentration on more powerful tools, such as quality function deployment, conjoint analysis, value engineering, design of experiments and benchmarking. Knowledge of these tools is essential to build up from a baseline level.

Design

Design of products and services should start by listening to the "voice of the customer," not the voice of the design engineer or management. In addition, the assessment should include the extent to which there are design processes to achieve zero variation (beyond zero defects), zero field failures, minimal field service, built-in diagnostics, ergonomics, low cost and short cycle time.

Suppliers

Just as we cannot have happy customers without happy, productive employees, so we cannot have happy customers without key suppliers, who are encouraged to establish partnerships with a company along the same lines as the latter builds with its core customers. The baseline audit should assess the same adherence to partnership principles as is done with customers, along with the amount and quality of active, concrete help rendered to each side.

Manufacturing

From a customer's perspective, there are two major elements associated with the effectiveness of manufacturing: quality and cycle time. In the last 10 years, manufacturing quality has received a great deal of attention and experienced an appreciable amount of improvement. A cycle time focus is much newer, but with pull systems and just-in-time practices (replacing old MRP-2 systems), delinquencies in delivery to the customer have fallen.

Field Operations

This is where the rubber meets the road — where the customer is able to observe the company's products and services first hand. Baseline assessments should include packing and transportation; installation and operating instructions; and accuracy, completeness and timing of repair service.

Support Services

As product quality has steadily improved, customer dissatisfaction is increasingly centered on poor support service: billing errors, wrong destinations, a run-around on inquiries, unsatisfactory problem resolution and — worse — lack of attention.

STEP 2: INTERNAL BENCHMARKING – ESTABLISHING A BASELINE

			RATING 1 2 3 4 5
A.		**Measurement**	
	1.	The number of defecting customers as a percent of the total number of customers is less than 5%.	
	2.	The longevity of core customers retained is measured in years.	
	3.	The value added for each core customer is measured by core customers themselves.	
	4.	The cost of poor quality, as measured by the accounting department, is analyzed and reduced.	
	5.	The hidden costs of poor quality are attempting to be quantified.	
	6.	The cycle times of key processes – manufacturing, design, businesses – are being measured and systematically reduced.	
B.		**Management** (see audit in Step 6)	
C.		**People**	
	1.	There is a climate of full trust between management and employees.	
	2.	Employees are not afraid to speak out, generate ideas and even constructively criticize management.	

THE CUSTOMER LOYALTY AUDIT

		RATING				
		1	2	3	4	5
3.	Employees are given regular feedback on their performance, especially as their activities affect customers.					
4.	Employees are given increasing responsibility in administering and managing their work areas.					
5.	Employees are given financial incentives based on their performance; and employees perceive that they have "a piece of the action" and a stake in the success of the company.					
6.	Customer-contact employees are given discretion to win over dissatisfied customers, including financial compensation within limits.					
D.	**Organization**					
1.	The organization chart is de-emphasized to prevent a vertical silo mentality and turf wars; and the team concept – especially cross-functional teams – is encouraged and nurtured.					
2.	A top management person is designated as the customer's advocate, either as an ombudsman or as the Chief Customer Officer (CCO).					
3.	The internal customer is elevated to a scorekeeper and evaluator of an internal supplier Performance appraisals are determined more by the internal customer and less by the supervisor.					
E.	**System**					
1.	Policies and procedures of little or no consequence to the customer are de-emphasized or eliminated.					
2.	The hiring of employees includes tests for the candidate's potential as a team player and for customer sensitivity.					
3.	Employee evaluations are based on team rather than individual performance					
4.	Small, automatic and annual merit raises are discarded in favor of more substantial bonuses, based on value added to the customer and fulfillment of goals.					
5.	Promotions are based on ability and potential for growth, rather than on past performance.					
F.	**Tools**					
1.	Quality function deployment, conjoint analysis, value research and allied tools are regularly used to capture the "voice of the customer."					
2.	Design of experiments (DOE)[17] is used to translate customer requirements into engineering specifications and tolerances and to parts specification and tolerances for suppliers.					
3.	Multiple environment overstress tests (MEOST)[18] are used to assure that field reliability for customers moves toward zero field failures.					
4.	Value engineering[19] is used to reduce costs to customers and simultaneously add value to customers – as perceived by them.					
5.	Benchmarking[20] is used to close the gap between the company and a best-in-class company in terms of a product or technique or function or department.					
6.	Total productive maintenance is used to improve process yields, up-time and efficiency.					

			RATING
			1 | 2 | 3 | 4 | 5
G.		**Design**	
	1.	Customers are systematically consulted before the start of a design to determine their most important needs and requirements and requested to compare the company against its best competition on each requirement.	
	2.	Reverse engineering or competitive analysis is used to compare the company's design versus its best competition in terms of features, materials, manufacturing, reliability and cost.	
	3.	Techniques to achieve zero variation[21] such as design of experiments, are used at the prototype stage of design.	
	4.	Techniques to achieve zero field failure,[22] such as multiple environment overstress tests, are used at the prototype stage of design.	
	5.	Design for manufacturability methods[23] are systematically employed to simplify manufacturing of the designs and quantify their manufacturability.	
	6.	Built-in diagnostics are designed to facilitate ease of repair, preferably by the customer directly.	
	7.	Ergonomics are considered to make the product or service user-friendly.	
	8.	Product/service liability prevention techniques[24] are employed to prevent danger to the customer as well as lawsuits.	
	9.	Cycle time reduction techniques are used to design the product/service in a fraction of the time used in older designs.	
	10.	Cost targeting, group technology and value engineering techniques are used.	
	11.	Concurrent engineering is used to use a cross-functional team approach during the entire design cycle.	
H.		**Suppliers**[25]	
	1.	A win–win partnership is established with key suppliers as a key corporate strategy.	
	2.	This partnership is sustained with uncompromising ethics, and full trust on both sides.	
	3.	Active, concrete and mutual help is rendered by both the company and its partnership suppliers for mutual benefit.	
	4.	A continuous price reduction for the company is targeted along with an increased profitability for partnership suppliers.	
I.		**Manufacturing**	
	1.	Key process parameters are characterized and optimized, using design of experiments, to achieve a minimum Cp of 2.0 (Cp is defined as the specification width divided by the process width of a given parameter).	
	2.	Key process parameters are "frozen," with Positrol,[25] to ensure optimized parameters stay within their pre-determined limits.	
	3.	Key quality peripherals, such as metrology, environments, configuration control, change control, are kept under tight control, using process certification.[26]	
	4.	Operator-controllable errors are prevented using poka yoke[27] methods.	

		RATING
		1 | 2 | 3 | 4 | 5
5.	Cycle time reduction is used to move manufacturing toward pull systems, focused factories, total productive maintenance (TPM), small lots, reduced set-up times and dedicated equipment and people.	
J.	**Field Operations**	
1.	Packing and transportation practices are reviewed to make sure the customer receives product with no damage or delay.	
2.	Installation and operating instructions are made understandable and user-friendly.	
3.	Customer understanding of applying the company's product or service is achieved through training, videotapes, seminars and personal visits by competent technical people.	
4.	Feedback is sought from the customer on the accuracy, completeness and timing of repair service.	
K.	**Support Services**	
1.	Business process improvements[28] are the norm, utilizing cross-functional teams, flow charts, mapping and "out-of-box" thinking.	
2.	The next "operation as customer"[29] is firmly established, whereby the internal customer – rather than the boss – evaluates an internal supplier (individual or team).	
3.	Non-product customer issues, such as billing errors, accounts receivable, access to key supplier personnel, speedy resolution of complaints or concerns, are courteously, promptly and completely addressed.	
4.	Attention to customers and their needs is paid long after sales.	

Total Maximum Score = 55 Factors x 5 = 275 Points

Step 3

DETERMINING CUSTOMER REQUIREMENTS

This step focuses on several methods of determining customer requirements. The prevalent practice until a decade ago was for management or engineering to gaze into their crystal ball to figure out what their customers wanted. The trouble was the crystal ball was murky. Even worse, management and their engineers, in their arrogance, believed they knew more of what their customers wanted than the customers themselves. The result was 80 percent of new products failed in the marketplace. As the vice-president of a major corporation used to say: "You may have the best dog food in the world, but if the dogs don't eat it, what good is it?"

Market Research

Many companies, in their attempt to graduate from products developed in isolation and then thrust down the customer's throat with slick advertising, have turned to market research as the "answer." It is only a slightly less cloudy crystal ball. It only researches the demographics associated with customers. It asks: "How did you hear about us?" and other peripheral questions. It does not ask: "What major experiences influenced your decision to try our product or service?" It does not research why a customer has defected. Further, it is done in isolation by sales-oriented personnel, who lack the depth of disciplines such as quality, product design and service. It is not a team exercise.

Market research's most memorable *faux pas* include the Edsel car, a stupendous piece of market research ending in Ford Motor Company's worst launch fiasco; and the more recent case of Dove, an ice-cream bar, panned by market research but a meteoric success in the marketplace.

Powerful Tools for Determining Customer Requirements

Fortunately, much better methods for taking the pulse of customer requirements have been developed over the last 20 years. Space permits only a brief description of each method.

Value Research[30]

A core group of potential customers representing the center of gravity of the larger customer population are given a product to evaluate. They keep track of their experiences and report back their strong dislikes, their strong likes and their "neutrals," i.e. features about which they are indifferent. The company then corrects the strong dislikes, advertises and promotes the strong likes and value engineers the unimportant features to reduce costs. Value research, while simple in concept, is powerful in its effectiveness.

Customer Window Model

This is a plot of product features and customer requirements with two axes. The first is the customer "gets" or "does not get" axis. The second is the "customer wants" versus "does not want" axis. This produces four quadrants, as shown in Figure 7. A concentration of the company's features in the lower right quadrant is overkill, a waste. A concentration in the upper left is a danger signal. A concentration in the upper right quadrant is the ideal.

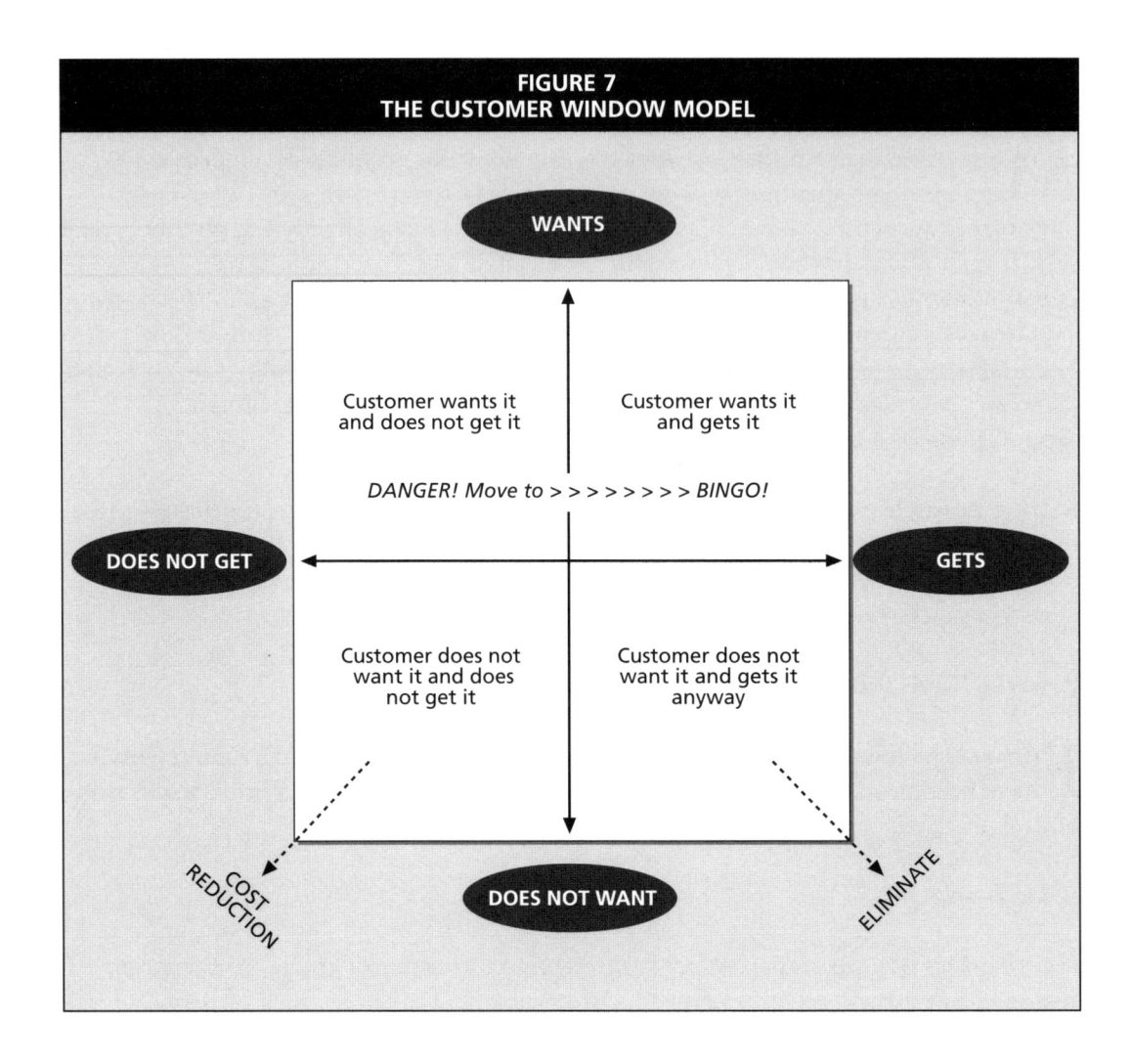

**FIGURE 7
THE CUSTOMER WINDOW MODEL**

WANTS

Customer wants it and does not get it	Customer wants it and gets it

DANGER! Move to > > > > > > > > BINGO!

DOES NOT GET ←→ GETS

Customer does not want it and does not get it	Customer does not want it and gets it anyway

COST REDUCTION

DOES NOT WANT

ELIMINATE

FIGURE 8
A 'DISCONNECT' BETWEEN A CUSTOMER'S IMPORTANCE OF VARIOUS REQUIREMENTS AND ITS SUPPLIER'S EMPHASIS

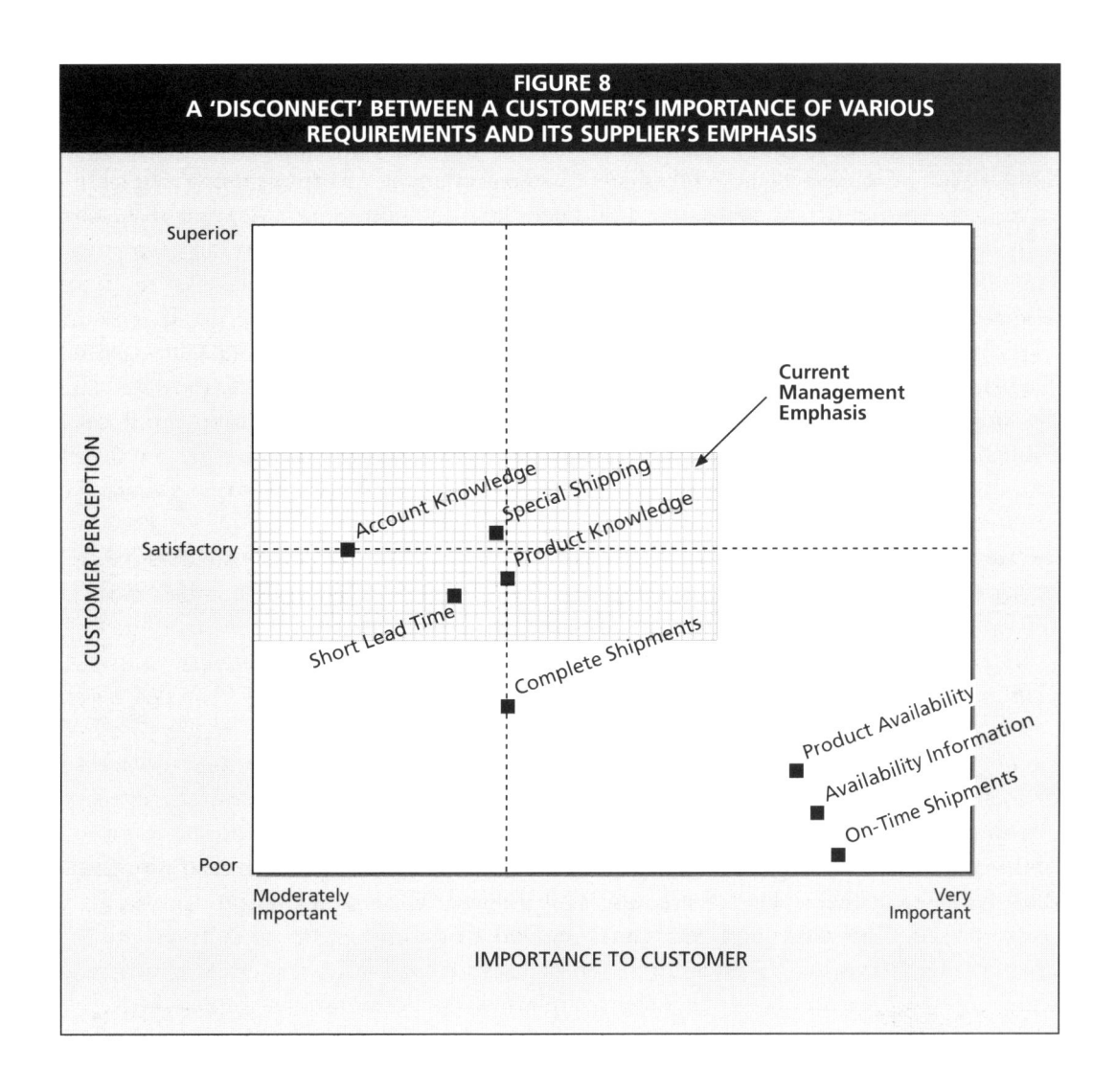

A variation of the customer window model is shown in Figure 8. This is based on a series of customer interviews for a consumer non-durables company.[31] It is a concise presentation of not only a customer's evaluation of various aspects of a supplier's performance, but also the apparent "disconnect" between the customer's important requirements and the emphasis placed by the supplier's management. Items important to the customer were rated poor, while the supplier's management emphasized requirements not very important to the customer.

Sensitivity Analysis[32]

This is another simple but powerful tool not exploited by most companies. Here, the level of each feature/requirement *vis-à-vis* its cost is examined in cooperation with core customers. If the gain in level was large for a relatively small increase in price, it would result in a mutual "go" decision. If, on the other hand, the gain in level was small for a large increase in cost and price, it would be a "no go."

Similarly, if a decrease in the level of a feature/requirement was small relative to a large decrease in cost and price, it would be a "go" decision. If vice versa, it would be a "no go."

Multi-Attribute Evaluation[33]

This is a matrix with the horizontal leg listing the various features of the product as determined by the customer and the vertical leg listing companies, including your own company and its best competitors. Each feature is given an importance scale, say from 1 to 10. Each company is then rated by customers for each feature, also on a scale, say from 1 to 5. The weighted rating in each box is the product of the importance of the feature multiplied by the company rating. The weighted ratings are then added up horizontally to determine the best company overall. Each feature is also scrutinized vertically to see how a company compares with its competition.

Conjoint Analysis

Conjoint analysis combines several features and presents them to potential customers or focus groups as a single option. There are also other options, each combining alternative levels of each of the above features. The customers can choose between options, but not cherry-pick a feature level in another option. Conjoint analysis has the advantage of segmenting customers, with different tastes and varying pocketbooks. It also has the advantage of limited models for the manufacturer and greater standardization. As an example, in the days when consumers could choose a wide variety of features in the cars they purchased, the permutations were endless. The Ford LTD, with a number of different features customers could choose, had 64,000 cars, with no car exactly like another. By contrast, the Honda Accord had only 400 models! Today, the Big Three have learnt the lessons of combining options for greater commonalty, if not standardization.

Quality Function Deployment[34] *(QFD)*

First introduced in Japan in the Kobe shipyards in 1970, QFD was introduced to the West in the mid-1980s. There are now over 10,000 companies in the US and Europe dabbling in QFD — dabbling, because they have not captured the greatest mileage from this powerful technique. (The automotive companies are probably furthest along in implementing QFD.) If done right, quality function deployment can help a company design products in half the time, with half the manpower, with half the defects and with half the costs and — at the same time — best quantify and prioritize customer requirements.

At first glance, the "House of Quality" matrix that results from QFD appears to be complicated. But with an hour or two of coaching, it can easily be demystified. Figure 9 is an example of a QFD on paper for a computer printer. The two left columns indicate customer requirements (the what) and the importance of each requirement. The vertical columns on top (the how) reflect these customer requirements translated into engineering specifications. The middle (large) section is a relationship matrix quantifying the strength of the relationship between each customer requirement and its corresponding engineering specification. The right column compares the customer's rating of the company, for each requirement, *vis-à-vis* the competition. The lower portions of the House of Quality indicate the target value of each engineering specification and how well they compare (see technical evaluation) to competition's specifications. The roof of the house shows how well each engineering specification is positively or negatively correlated to other specifications.

The objectives of this study are to:

- ascertain and prioritize customer requirements before a new design begins — in other words, capturing the voice of the customer rather than the voice of the engineer

- obtain the customer's view of the company's strengths and weaknesses *vis-à-vis* its competition on each customer requirement

- compare the company's strengths and weaknesses *vis-à-vis* its competition on each engineering specification, through reverse engineering (i.e. competitive analysis)

- highlight incompatibilities in design (negative correlations)

- and, as the bottom line, pinpoint the important, the new and the difficult in the preliminary design.

Reading the Customer's Mind

Even with the power of QFD, the question remains: how do you really fathom what is in customers' minds — their needs, their expectations, their requirements? There are many techniques for this, a few effective, but most marginal. The latter include listening at trade shows; 800 numbers where customers can call in toll free; "quickie" cards mailed to customers with their product and soliciting their comments at the first point of usage; mail surveys; and "hidden" surveys, where the name of the company requesting the survey is withheld from customers, generally conducted through an intermediary such as a consultant. These methods do generate some information about customer requirements, but this is for the most part filtered information obtained through indirect contact with customers. With some of the

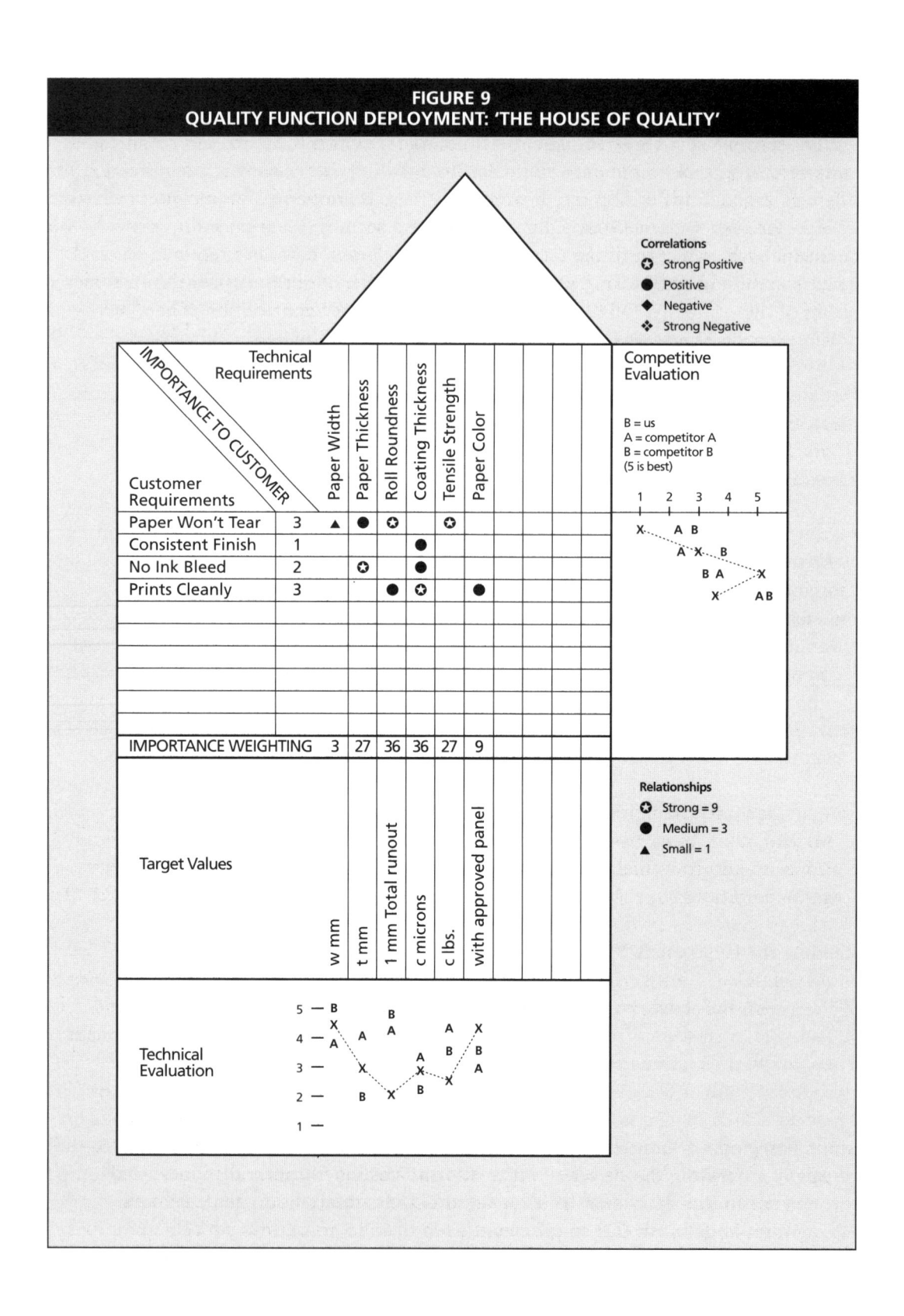

FIGURE 9
QUALITY FUNCTION DEPLOYMENT: 'THE HOUSE OF QUALITY'

Correlations
- ✪ Strong Positive
- ● Positive
- ◆ Negative
- ✤ Strong Negative

Customer Requirements	Importance to Customer	Paper Width	Paper Thickness	Roll Roundness	Coating Thickness	Tensile Strength	Paper Color
Paper Won't Tear	3	▲	●	✪		✪	
Consistent Finish	1				●		
No Ink Bleed	2		✪		●		
Prints Cleanly	3			●	✪		●
IMPORTANCE WEIGHTING		3	27	36	36	27	9

Competitive Evaluation

B = us
A = competitor A
B = competitor B
(5 is best)

1 2 3 4 5

Target Values
- w mm
- t mm
- 1 mm Total runout
- c microns
- c lbs.
- with approved panel

Relationships
- ✪ Strong = 9
- ● Medium = 3
- ▲ Small = 1

Technical Evaluation

above techniques it is also too late: the product or service is already in the customers' hands.

There are, however, three very effective techniques:

Focus Groups, Clinics, Panels

Typical representatives of the center of gravity of the projected customer population are assembled by the company to solicit their opinions and recommendations on "clay" models or prototypes of the product or service being launched. The discussions are led by a trained facilitator or observed by key company personnel behind a one-way glass panel. The advantages are instant feedback, as well as a determination of consensus or diversity of opinions. The disadvantage is a "herd mentality" may develop, where a dominant person may pull the rest of the panel into a forced agreement or panel members may be hesitant to speak their true minds.

Customer Contact Personnel Inputs

Employees who frequently come into contact with customers can be a very good source of information. Even though this source is best utilized after the product or service is in the field, the inputs, ideas and recommendations of customer-contact employees can be most useful on older products or services, as they may affect newer products or services.

One-On-One In-Depth Interviews

None of the above techniques can come close to the information gained from spending time with customers themselves, one on one, in their own environment. This may be time consuming and costly to do, but it is certainly in order for core customers who constitute only 20 percent by number but 80 percent by sales volume.

Interviews should be conducted not only with people in a customer organization who make purchasing decisions, but with actual users who "feel the product, smell the product, deal in the product." Most face-to-face interviews should last one to one-and-a-half hours. The interviewer should let the customer describe — without structure or prompting at first — the key product or service attributes which would lead to increased purchases or cause purchases to decline. In some cases, managers from the company may conduct the interviews. For others, outside support may be preferable, using "blind" interviewers, not identified with a specific company, in order to get unbiased responses.

Interviews generally continue until key responses are consistently repeated and until unique responses describe exceptional or unusual customers' responses. This is likely to happen after about 12 to 15 interviews.

THE CUSTOMER LOYALTY AUDIT

If You Don't Learn the Lessons of History, You Are Likely to Repeat Your Mistakes

The great majority of companies display a fundamental weakness in their search for customer requirements: they concentrate only on existing customers or on new ones. They do not poll former customers or non-customers. Former customers, who have defected, can provide a wealth of information about their disenchantment with the company. Non-customers likewise — although harder to identify — can stipulate the reasons they were never enticed to try the company's products or services. A concerted effort should be made, again using the one-on-one interview technique if possible, to touch these two important bases.

STEP 3: DETERMINING CUSTOMER REQUIREMENTS

		RATING 1 2 3 4 5
A.	**Poor Methods Not to Be Used for Determining Customer Requirements**	
1.	Management and engineering do not use the "voice of the engineer" in assuming they know customer requirements better than the customer.	
2.	Slick and false advertising is forbidden to lure unwary customers.	
3.	Market research is used only peripherally to determine customer demographics, not as a sure-fire way of determining customer requirements.	
B.	**Modern Techniques to Gauge the Pulse of Customer Requirements**	
1.	One or more of the following methods are used to determine customer requirements: value research; window model; sensitivity analysis; multi-attribute evaluation; conjoint analysis.	
2.	The use of quality function deployment (QFD) is encouraged as one of the best ways to determine the "voice of the customer."	
3.	The 2nd and 3rd cascades of QFD are also employed to translate engineering specifications into part, process and test specifications.	
C.	**Probing the Customers' Minds to Determine Needs and Expectations**	
1.	Focus groups, clinics and panels are used as one input.	
2.	Customer-contact employees' inputs, ideas and recommendations are sought systematically as another input.	
3.	One-on-one in-depth interviews are conducted with core customers as the best and most systematic way of determining customer needs, requirements and expectations.	
4.	Former and non-customers are eagerly sought to round out the above perspective.	

Step 4

ASSESSING THE CAPABILITIES OF COMPETITION

Sun Tsu, a brilliant Chinese general, wrote in 500 BC: "If you know your enemy and know yourself, you need not fear the result of a hundred battles."

The previous steps have established a baseline. This steps helps you to "know your enemy," in modern terms your competition. It details a number of techniques by which the capabilities of the company's best competitor can be assessed and the gap between the two companies — in terms of customer satisfaction and loyalty — quantified.

Quality Function Deployment (QFD)

A brief description of quality function deployment was given in Step 3. In the "House of Quality" matrix the right side is devoted to a rating by the customer of how a company compares against two of its best competitors on each of the customer's important requirements. The usual scale is 1 to 5, with 1 being the worst and 5 the best.

The bottom portion of the QFD matrix is another assessment of the same two competitors, this time performed by the company. This reverse engineering, or competitive evaluation, process compares how each engineering parameter of the company (the "how" in the matrix) is rated — on a scale of 1 to 5, with 1 being the worst and 5 the best — against these best competitors. As a result of these comprehensive evaluations, the company has a much clearer and more quantitative comparison of its strengths and weaknesses *vis-à-vis* competition.

Benchmarking[35]

Besides internal benchmarking, detailed in Step 2, two other types of benchmarking should be pursued. The first is competitive benchmarking, determining who is the best competitor. The second is generic benchmarking, determining which is the best company, preferably a non-competitor possibly even better than a competitor.

Applied to the discipline of customer service, both types of benchmarking processes are in order. Competitive benchmarking has the advantage of directly comparing the customer service process between two companies with similar products, services and customers. As a disadvantage, the competitor benchmark company may not cooperate in the study and could regard its customer service as highly proprietary. Generic benchmarking has the advantage of much easier access to and cooperation by the benchmark company, since it is not a competitor. Time permitting, both types of benchmarking should be pursued, so the company gets two perspectives on best practices associated with customer service.

Industry Reports

Other important sources of competitive performance are various reports published in the media:

- J.D. Powers' reports on customer satisfaction with cars are well known, widely read and authentic. They are taken very seriously by the automotive companies, who seldom fail to use them in their advertising — when favorable. J.D. Powers also performs comparative evaluations of companies in several other businesses.

- Government reports compare airlines on accident rates, on-time arrivals and lost baggage.

- Consumer magazines rate various products and are frequently consulted by customers in their buying decisions. But there can be nagging questions about slants in the questionnaires, sample sizes, evaluation techniques and data shading.

- Commissioned studies are conducted on a wide variety of products, companies, universities and hospitals, rating them annually.

Independent Laboratories

Laboratories are often used by companies to perform product evaluations. Most of these render above-board service, but there is always the danger that the one who pays the piper gets to call the tune!

STEP 4: ANALYZING CAPABILITIES OF COMPETITION

		RATING 1 2 3 4 5
1.	Quality function deployment is systematically used, whereby the core customers rate the company against its best competitors on each important customer requirement.	
2.	The company performs reverse engineering on its competitor's products or services and compares each engineering specification against its competitor and against a target value for that specification.	
3.	The company benchmarks its customer service process against its best competitor.	
4.	The company benchmarks its customer service process against non-competing companies with the best reputations for such service	
5.	The company utilizes a variety of industry reports to compare its products and services against competition.	
6.	The company utilizes independent laboratories and/or outside consultants to compare its products and services against competition.	

Step 5

MEASURING CUSTOMER SATISFACTION AND CUSTOMER LOYALTY

Product quality is relatively easy to measure: outgoing quality, field reliability yields, total defects per unit, Cp and Cpk, etc. These are objective, quantifiable parameters and progress can easily be tracked over time. Service quality is harder to measure, except for field repairs. Its parameters are more subjective and less quantifiable.

Customer satisfaction is even harder to measure, because it depends largely on the human element. Customer satisfaction is what the customer says it is. But customer loyalty, on the other hand — while far more important — is actually easier to quantify at a given time period, as well as longitudinally over time, because it is based on what the customer *does*.

This step deals with the various methods of measuring customer satisfaction as well as customer loyalty. A grade has been assigned to each metric, reflecting its overall effectiveness, with D as a failing grade and A and A plus as excellent.

Customer Satisfaction Metrics – Indirect Measures

Warranty Costs (D minus)

Most companies track their warranty costs, usually as a percentage of sales. But not only is this a catastrophic indication of customer dissatisfaction, it comes too late. Further, it is only the tip of the iceberg. The company has no idea of failures after the warranty period (for the most part only one year), much larger in number and more serious in terms of customer dissatisfaction than in-warranty failures. Customers feel they are being hung out to dry.

Customer Complaints/Claims (D)

This is an important statistic but, as in the case of warranty costs, it comes too late. The damage is already done. Many companies, instead of correcting the problems, hide behind excuses such as "No trouble found" where the failure could not be confirmed; customer misuse; customer's lack of knowledge in operating the product or service; and, in a few cases, even customer fraud. These excuses are sleeping pills. When the company wakes up, it may well be out of business.

Market Share: (C)

Popular as a measure of company performance, market share is not an accurate gauge of customer satisfaction and is even more nebulous as a gauge of customer loyalty. It measures the quantity not the quality of a company's services to its customers. It does not distinguish between new customers and old customers, nor does it distinguish between one-time customers and lifetime customers. It only compares the company against its competitors. It does not determine whether the market as a whole is growing in importance or is fading. And there is also the "sleeper effect," where market share may be maintained for a few quarters but unexpectedly plunges because of cumulative customer dissatisfaction over time.

Cost of Poor Quality (B)

This metric has been explained in detail in Step 2. It could be an excellent metric (and upgraded to A) if the cost of a defecting customer can be estimated, as outlined in that step. But 99 percent of companies do not even know about this colossal loss, much less estimate it.

Industry Reports (B)

This subject has been covered in Step 4. Of the many types of such reports, the ones issued by J.D. Powers are the fairest, most accurate and most eagerly tracked by the affected companies.

Business Statistics

In addition to the above measures, there are a number of ways in which customer satisfaction can be measured with business statistics:

- *Ratio of sales wins to sales losses* (B) – by volume, by sales dollars and longitudinally over time.

- *Capture ratio* (B minus) – the ratio of new customers to the number of proposals to win them.

- *Conversion efficiency* (B minus) — the number of new customers per dollar of investment.

- *Mean time between winning a customer and losing that customer* (B minus).

Customer satisfaction index (B):

$$S/I_1 - LS/I_2$$

where

S = Sales from satisfied customers
I_1 = Investment to assure satisfied customers
LS = Lost sales from dissatisfied customers
I_2 = Investment to save dissatisfied customers

Business statistics have their advantages. They are quantified and can show trends over time. Management understands them, is sensitive to them and can use them to initiate corrective action. The disadvantages of such statistics are the numerous variables affecting customer satisfaction or dissatisfaction, hard to pinpoint as root causes.

Direct Customer Surveys

There is no better method of measuring customer satisfaction than asking customers themselves for their evaluation. Common to several techniques is the questionnaire. A poorly designed questionnaire, whether for mail or telephone surveys, will be the source of misleading feedback from customers.

Questionnaire Design Dos and Don'ts

- Keep the questionnaire short, easy to fill out and user friendly. It should not take up more than 15 minutes of a customer's time. The questions should not be ambiguous or difficult to understand and interpret.

- Let customers, not managers, select the parameters important to them. A major health insurer felt speed of answer, tone of response and accuracy were important to customers. But what most customers wanted was clarity of explanation and the reassurance their problem would be resolved.

- Select no more than 10 to 15 parameters for the questionnaire, associated with those elements of customer satisfaction most important to customers. (Use the results of a QFD study, if possible, to determine importance.) The more the parameters, the greater the customer's dilemma in rating each of them and the more difficult the analysis. American Express uses 180 parameters to measure customer satisfaction. This is overkill, expensive and ineffective. On the opposite side of the spectrum, companies like Caterpillar Service, Auto Spark and Kroger (for its suppliers) concentrate on just one parameter — speed of delivery. Caterpillar prides itself on being able to dispatch a service part to any location in the world within 48 hours. Auto Spark, with an inventory of 30,000 parts, can deliver a part to a customer anywhere in the US within one day.

- Include truly important questions, such as:

  - Would you buy this product (or service) again?

  - Would you buy a product of the same brand name (i.e. other products made by the same company)?

  - Would you recommend this product (or service) to a friend?

  - How can we serve you better?

- Allow time and space for responses.

- Use professionals with a proven track record (either within the company or outside consultants) to design the questionnaire.

- In telephone or person-to-person surveys, use trained interviewers who are sensitive to customers — their moods, their frustrations or their enthusiasm.

- Where possible, use outsiders because customers are more frank with them than with a company interviewer.

Mail Surveys (D)

While cheaper and quicker than other methods, these generate the poorest response from customers, generally less than 10 to 15 percent. They are impersonal, provide only one-way communication and tend to be skewed towards complaining customers who may use the survey instrument to vent their feelings.

Telephone Surveys (C)

These are more expensive than mail surveys, but they provide two-way communications with the customer and allow emotional factors to be registered. The disadvantages are: targeted customers are often difficult to reach; the public is inundated with them and often resent them; and the all-important body language signals are absent.

Focus Groups, Clinics, Panels (B plus)

These have been discussed in Step 3 in the context of determining customer requirements. They are also an excellent forum for measuring customer satisfaction.

The addition of former customers as well as non-customers to such groups is highly desirable, because they could highlight the negatives associated with the company's products or services.

Soliciting Non-Customer Inputs (B plus)

This is seldom done. But asking non-customers how satisfied they are with various features and aspects of a competitor's product or service affords a company a benchmarking perspective. Their inputs are valuable sources for improving the company's own performance.

Soliciting Former Customer Inputs (A)

Seeking feedback only from existing customers is tantamount to "preaching to the converted." Companies miss a trick by not polling former customers, either singly or collectively in a forum, to understand the reasons for their disenchantment. Such encounters may actually help in recapturing former customers.

Customer-Contact Employee Inputs (A)

These have also been discussed in Step 3. Customer-contact employees are in frequent touch with customers. Jan Carlson, dynamic chairman of SAS Airlines, calls these contacts "fifty million moments of truth." Yet a myopic management seldom solicits their opinions, ideas and suggestions. How often, when customers complain about a service, is there a kneejerk response from an employee, suggesting they write to the company. "Management won't listen to us," they lament. Customers then react: "We've written to your management. They don't listen to us either." Progressive companies regularly tap this vast reservoir of employee knowledge of customers — their gripes, their preferences, their suggestions for improvement.

One-on-One Interviews (A plus)

This is the most expensive and time-consuming approach and is best limited to the core customers who represent less than 20 percent of the total customer base, but constitute more than 80 percent of total sales. Such customers deserve individual attention, with in-depth interviews described in Step 3. The interviewees should be those within the customer company who make or influence the purchasing decisions as well as the actual users of the supplier company's product or services. The interviewers should be members of the supplier company's senior management or outside agencies and consultants with whom customers are less likely to pull their punches.

Frequency of Polling

The number of times customers are polled to determine satisfaction varies with different products and services and with different types of customers. Once a year appears too long an interval for most companies to analyze and improve performance. AT&T used to be comfortable with an annual survey because of the nature of its business. Its customers, in the monopoly heydays, could not jump ship. But with the speed and intensity of new competitors, including its own Baby Bells, its polling frequency is now much higher. At the other extreme is Federal Express, with a frequency of once a month. Its volume of business and the number of steps in its delivery cycle warrant more frequent polling. A general rule of thumb is once per quarter.

However, for core customers polling should be more or less continuous. Core customers need close and constant attention. Their changing needs, requirements and expectations must be carefully monitored and addressed. And personal contacts are vital if there is to be a climate of mutual trust and help.

Customer Loyalty Metrics

Customer loyalty is easier to measure than customer satisfaction — the polling and the voting are done with the customers' feet. There are several measures:

- *Maintenance Ratio (A)* – Ratio of the number of current customers retained to the number who have defected.

- *Defection Rate (A plus)* – The number of customers who have defected as a percentage of the total number of customers. Any figure over 10 percent should be cause for pushing the panic button.

- *Amount and Continuity of Core Customers (A plus)* – By number, by dollars and by time.

- *Longevity of Core Customers (A plus)* – Total sales generated by long-term customers over several years is an excellent measure of customer loyalty.

- *Value to Core Customer (A plus)* – Saving dollars for core customers in terms of quality, cost, cycle time, productivity, etc. (especially over time) is, or should be, a company's main objective. Preferably, this metric should be developed in conjunction with the customer. It promotes mutual loyalty and mutual profit.

THE CUSTOMER LOYALTY AUDIT

STEP 5: MEASURING CUSTOMER SATISFACTION AND LOYALTY

			RATING
			1 | 2 | 3 | 4 | 5
A.	**Quality Metrics**		
1.	The company systematically measures plant quality, with parameters such as outgoing quality; total defects per unit; yields/cycle time charts; and Cp, Cpk for individual product/process characteristics.		
2.	The company systematically measures field reliability, with parameters such as warranty costs, claims, complaints.		
3.	The company systematically gathers the cost of poor quality – including the cost and longevity of customer defections.		
4.	The company systematically measures the cost of retrofits, recalls, product liability suits and legal costs associate with the settlement of such suits.		
B.	**Industry and Independent Reports**		
1.	The company utilizes industry reports, such as JD Powers, government and university sources to determine customer satisfaction *vis-à-vis* its competition.		
2.	The company utilizes reports by magazines, such as *Consumer Union*, to determine an evaluation of the company's product or services *vis-à-vis* its competition.		
3.	The company commissions independent laboratories to compare its products against those of its competition.		
C.	**Business Statistics**		
1.	The company uses several business statistics, such as ratio of sales wins to sales losses, customer satisfaction index, etc. to measure customer satisfaction.		
D.	**Direct Customer Surveys**		
1.	The company uses a survey instrument where the customer, rather than the company, selects the parameters of customer satisfaction to be measured.		
2.	The total number of parameters measured are those most important to the customer and do not exceed a maximum of 15.		
3.	The survey instrument always includes the following questions: • "Would you buy this product (or service) again?" • "Would you buy a product of the same brand name?" • "Would you recommend this product (or service) to a friend?" • "How can we serve you better?"		

The Customer Loyalty Audit

		RATING
		1 | 2 | 3 | 4 | 5
4.	The company de-emphasizes mail and telephone surveys and concentrates instead on one-on-one surveys for its core customers.	
5.	The company solicits inputs on its products and services regularly from former customers and on its competitor's products and services from non-customers.	
6.	The company regularly taps the knowledge of its customer-contact employees in determining customer satisfaction.	
7.	The company uses business statistics, such as the defection rate of customers, to measure customer loyalty.	
8.	The company measures loyalty of its core customers by their number, by dollars and by time.	
9.	The company measures loyalty of its core customers by the value core customers perceive they have received from the company.	

Step **6**

ANALYZING CUSTOMER AND COMPETITIVE FEEDBACK

Once customer satisfaction and loyalty have been measured against customer requirements, feedback from customers, competition, former customers and non-customers should be analyzed. Several pitfalls should be avoided.

- Sticking to a particular questionnaire, even though the response from customers is poor or — based on customer comments — is inadequate or inappropriate.

- Not changing a survey format in order to track performance over time, even though the format needs to be revised and updated.

- Gathering so much data — relevant and non-relevant — you can't see the forest for the trees. Data pollution is a common weakness in many customer satisfaction surveys.

- No follow-up. This is the worst scenario, caused by disbelief in the data, political infighting within the company, lack of management support or external conditions checkmating corrective action.

- Using results incorrectly. An example of this is a reward system based on survey results for individuals and/or departments only remotely connected to the customer.

- Combining "satisfied" and "very satisfied" ratings as a single measure of favorable customer responses. Several surveys use a variable rating scale of 1 to 5 to measure customer satisfaction, with 1 representing "very dissatisfied," 2 "dissatisfied," 3 "neutral," 4 "satisfied" and 5 "very satisfied." A common mistake companies make is adding up the 4s and the 5s (some take this addition and divide it by the 1s and 2s added together) to arrive at a measure of overall satisfaction. This is dangerous. A company can only take comfort in a score preponderantly made up of 5s — respondents with a 4 are likely to defect!

As an example, a major telecommunications retailer conducted a satisfaction survey.[36] It asked: "What do you think of our customer service?" The results are shown in Table 2. The survey followed up with another question: "Would you return to us the next time you need telecommunications equipment?" Of those who indicated the service was average, 46 percent would not buy there again. Of those who indicated the service was good, a whopping 30 percent would not buy there again. But of those who indicated the service was excellent, only 2 percent would not return to the company.

TABLE 2
RELATIONSHIP BETWEEN CUSTOMER SATISFACTION AND CUSTOMER RETENTION

SATISFACTION RATING	% CUSTOMERS RESPONDING	% CUSTOMERS RETURNING YES	NO
Excellent	2%	98%	2%
Good	13%	70%	30%
Fair	62%	54%	46%
Poor	23%	3%	97%

Developing a Single Customer Satisfaction Index

A prevalent practice in industry is to develop a single overall score — generally from 1 to 100 — to integrate and quantify various business parameters. The development of a single score to combine the many elements of customer satisfaction or enthusiasm listed in Figures 4 and 5 is similarly desirable to measure customer satisfaction.

One method this author has developed is illustrated in Figure 10. It is a generic model for products. The first column lists the specific requirements the core customers consider essential. These requirements can be derived from a QFD study or through one-on-one interviews. The list should not be too long or too short. Generally, 10 to 15 parameters with top priorities as determined by the customer, not by the company, are the norm.

The second column depicts the importance (I) customers attach to each requirement on a scale of 1 to 5, with 1 having the lowest importance and 5 the highest. In the third column, customers rate the company's performance (R) for each requirement, again on the same scale of 1 to 5. The fourth column multiplies the figures in columns 2 and 3 to determine the company's score (S) = (I) × (R) for each requirement. To determine the overall customer satisfaction index (CSI), the importance numbers in column 2 are added (Y), as are the scores in column 4 (T). The overall index for customer satisfaction is T/5Y × 100, expressed as a percentage. (The reason for the 5Y in the denominator is that the maximum score a company can receive for each requirement is 5.)

THE CUSTOMER LOYALTY AUDIT

FIGURE 10
CUSTOMER SATISFACTION INDEX (CSI) GENERIC MODEL FOR PRODUCTS

REQUIREMENT	IMPORTANCE (I) SCALE: 1–5	CO. RATING (R) SCALE: 1–5	CO. SCORE (S) (S) = (I) x (R)	COMPETITOR RATING (CR) SCALE: 1–5	COMPETITOR SCORE (CS) SCALE: 1–5
Quality (upon receipt)					
Reliability (within warranty)					
Durability (lifetime)					
Serviceability					
Up-Time (% use)					
Tech. Performance					
Features (that sell)					
Safety					
Human Engineering					
Reputation					
Sales Cooperativeness					
Price					
Resale Price					
Delivery					
TOTAL SCORE	SUM OF (I) = (Y)		SUM OF (I) = (Y)		SUM OF (CS) = (U)

Customer Satisfaction Index (CSI) %

a) for company $= \frac{T}{5Y} \times 100$

b) for competitor $= \frac{U}{5Y} \times 100$

The same CSI can be expanded to determine how a company's best competitor is assessed by the customer. The fifth column is the customer's rating of the competitor's performance (CR) for each requirement, also on a scale of 1 to 5. The sixth column multiplies the numbers in columns 2 and 5 to determine a competitor's score (CS) = (I) × (CR) for each requirement. To determine an overall CSI for the competitor, the scores in column 6 (CS) are added (U). The overall CSI for the competitor is U/5Y × 100, also expressed as a percentage.

THE CUSTOMER LOYALTY AUDIT

FIGURE 11
CSI OF A COMPANY PROVIDING ENGINEERING
SERVICE ON CONTRACT (RATED BY THE OEM COMPANY CONTRACTING FOR THE SERVICE

REQUIREMENT	IMPORTANCE (I) SCALE: 1–5	CO. RATING (R) SCALE: 1–5	CO. SCORE (S) (S) = (I) x (R)	COMPETITOR RATING (CR) SCALE: 1–5	COMPETITOR SCORE (CS) SCALE: 1–5
Placements Speed	4	5	20	3	12
Placement Professionalism	5	4	20	2	10
Low Cost	4	2	8	5	20
Dependability	3	4	12	3	9
Flexibility	1	3	3	5	5
Cooperativeness	2	4	8	3	6
Reputation	3	4	12	5	15
	SUB TOT (Y) 22		SUB TOT (S) 83		SUB TOT (U) 77

Company CSI Index: $\frac{I}{5Y} \times 100 = \frac{83}{100} - 75 = 5\%$

Competitor company CSI Index: $\frac{U}{5Y} \times 100 = \frac{77}{100} = 70\%$

Figure 11 illustrates the use of a CSI where a large original equipment manufacturer (OEM) rated its supplier, who provided engineers to this company on a contract basis. It also rated a competitive supplier. While the overall CSIs were close for the two supplier companies, there were considerable differences between the two in the ratings for the individual requirements. For example, the company is superior to its competitor in two requirements very important to the customer — placement speed and placement professionalism. But its high-cost services need to be reduced. It also needs to enhance its reputation in the eyes of its customer.

The same CSI can also be used for internal customers. Figure 12 depicts how the sponsor of a training project rated an internal supplier team which designed the training manual. The overall CSI was a poor 53 percent (maximum score being 100 percent). But the team also received low scores for several individual requirements the internal customer deemed important.

THE CUSTOMER LOYALTY AUDIT

FIGURE 12
CSI OF A TEAM DESIGNING A
TRAINING MANUAL (RATED BY THE PROJECT SPONSOR)

REQUIREMENT	IMPORTANCE (I) SCALE: 1–10	RATING (R) SCALE: 1–5	SCORE (S) (S) = (I) x (R)		
1. Quality					
• Completeness	7	4	28		
• Accuracy	9	1	9		
• Clarity	8	3	24		
• Meaningfulness	10	2	20		
2. Timeliness					
• On-time Delivery	8	1	8		
• Cycle Time	5	1	5		
3. Cost (to customer)	6	3	18		
4. Dependability					
• Promises Kept	4	2	8		
• Credibility	6	3	18		
• Trustworthiness	7	2	14		
5. Cooperativeness					
• Responsiveness	5	4	20		
• Flexibility	4	3	12		
• Approachability	6	5	30		
• Courtesy	4	5	20		
6. Communication					
• Listening	4	4	16		
• Feed Forward	5	2	10		
• Information					
TOTAL SCORE	SUB 98 TOTAL (Y)		SUB 260 TOTAL (Y)		

Customer Satisfaction Index: $\frac{1}{5Y} \times 100 = \frac{260}{490} = 53\%$

The elegance of the customer satisfaction index is the remarkable way in which it simultaneously analyzes:

- the relative importance customers attach to their priority requirements

- the strengths and weaknesses of the company *vis-à-vis* those requirements, as determined by the customer

- the strengths and weaknesses of the company *vis-à-vis* its best competition, again as determined by the customer.

Analysis of Customer Defections

The great majority of companies are concerned only in a vague way about customer defections. A large percentage do not measure their customer defection rates and even among those companies which do, there is little analysis, using the Pareto principle, of the main reasons for such defections.

A world-class company constantly monitors its customer defection rates on a monthly basis, more often for its core customers. It analyzes the top causes for the defections and then mounts a massive effort to remedy such causes and win back defecting customers. It is estimated that a 5 percent reduction in defections can result in an 85 percent increase in profit — a neglected gold mine!

Analysis of Non-Customer Buying Habits

As in the case of customer defections, most companies do not explore why various segments of the market do not buy their products or services but select their competitors instead. This type of benchmarking can pay handsome dividends. Several vital causes can be unearthed:

- Little knowledge of the company or its products

- Poor quality and reliability as perceived by the public

- Poor public image

- Unfavorable mentions in the news media

- Product liability lawsuits and settlements

- Recall campaigns

- Disgruntled customers telling their friends and neighbors

- Dealer sales representatives pushing competitors' products or services

Use of Information Technology (IT)

Using information technology a complete profile of each core customer can be obtained — what products they buy, where they buy, how frequently etc. This information can be used to provide various preferential services to reward the core customer, such as advance information on sales, discounts, promotions.

The Concentration Decision

Finally, a company cannot afford to be of service to all customers. Strange as it may seem, not all customers are worth keeping:

- Dishonest customers may take advantage of generous company policies. For instance, one company euphemistically identifies these customers as "weekend" customers. They buy the company's tools for weekend use and return them to the dealer, with a variety of excuses, for full credit.

- Dissatisfied customers may perpetually complain, regardless of the triviality of the complaint or the accommodation extended to them by the company.

- Some customers may consistently seek to squeeze a company for price reductions without any redeeming characteristics to justify retaining them as customers.

- Other customers may buy only the tail-ends of a company's diversity of products or services in uneconomic quantities.

- Other customers are not profitable to the company or likely to develop into preferred or core customers. One company with which this author consulted had 800 customers. Of these, its accounting department confirmed almost 600 of them were not profitable. When asked why it kept the latter, the answer was "to keep the plant busy!" After much soul searching, the company did reduce its customer base by 25 percent. It began to serve its core customers better with this concentration decision and returned to profitability.

THE CUSTOMER LOYALTY AUDIT

STEP 6: ANALYZING CUSTOMER AND COMPETITIVE FEEDBACK

		RATING
		1 2 3 4 5

A. Survey Instrument Design

1. The company continually re-assesses its survey instruments, such as its questionnaires, to make sure they are adequate, relevant and customer-sensitive.

2. The company is not averse to changing a survey format (for fear of not tracking customer satisfaction progress if the baseline is changed).

B. Feedback Data Analysis

1. The company follows up customer feedback with professional analysis and improvement measures.

2. The company only uses the "very satisfied" or "excellent" ratings in determining customer loyalty.

3. The company uses an overall customer satisfaction index (CSI) to determine its strengths and weaknesses relative to its customers' important requirements.

4. The company uses an overall customer satisfaction index (CSI) to determine its strengths and weaknesses relative to its best competitors.

C. Former Customers
The company regularly analyzes the reasons for its customer defections and mounts a massive effort to win defecting customers back.

D. Non-Customers
The company regularly assesses the reasons why non-customers stay away from the company's products or services and institutes remedial actions.

E. Information Technology
The company utilizes information technology to obtain a complete profile of each core customer and attempts to provide preferential services to such customers.

F. Dropping Customers
The company identifies customers which need to be terminated in order to concentrate on preferred and core customers and enhance its own profitability.

Step 7

CONTINUOUS IMPROVEMENT

After customer and competitive feedback has been analyzed, the hard task of correcting the causes of customer complaints and customer dissatisfaction begins. Even if customers are satisfied, there is no guarantee they will be repeat customers. Their requirements need to be continually assessed. No efforts to continue to earn the loyalty of customers are too Herculean. In short, customer satisfaction and especially customer loyalty represent a journey without end. As is said frequently about quality, there is no finish line for customers.

This step concentrates on several facets of a continuous improvement process, starting with complaints and problems perceived by customers and the necessary corrective measures.

Causes and Remedies for Typical Customer Complaints

Customer complaints can be divided into a few broad categories. Table 3 lists the most typical areas of customer problems, their causes and the most appropriate tools and techniques to correct them. Strange as it may seem, many of those techniques are not even known to most companies, much less used by them.

As an example, a Fortune 500 company launched a 10:1 improvement drive for its field reliability. The objective was right on target, but the results were not. Halfway through this five-year goal, the company was one-and-a-half years behind in its timetable and losing ground each month. The corrective actions being taken were reminiscent of practices 20 years previously. The tools being used included Pareto prioritization, cause-and-effect diagrams, committees, finger pointing, responsibility transference to some other group, such as suppliers, design etc. With a sense of urgency, the company has now switched to powerful tools like multiple environment overstress tests and the design of experiments to solve these chronic field problems. It is well on its way to beating the original timetable — of a 10:1 improvement in five years — by a full year.

Management Audits

Especially in the service sector, management audits are used to monitor and improve the effectiveness of services rendered to customers. These may be announced or unannounced. Airline executives put themselves in a customer's shoes, starting with phoning for a reservation and monitoring the entire experience of waiting in line for a ticket, assessing gate procedures, flight service and courtesy, and

TABLE 3
TYPICAL CUSTOMER-REPORTED PROBLEMS, THEIR CAUSES AND CORRECTIVE TOOLS

AREA	CAUSES	APPROPRIATE CORRECTIVE TOOLS
Poor product quality	• Poor design • Poor manufacturing • Poor material from suppliers • Poor workmanship	• Design of experiments (DOE) • Design of experiments; Total productive maintenance (TPM) • Design of experiments • Poka yoke
Poor product reliability	Designs not robust with time and field stresses	Multiple environment overstress testing (MEOST) and DOE
Product liability potential	• Poor design for human and product safety • Customer misapplication	• Product liability prevention (PLP) • Misapplication-proof design; warning label
Poor field repair service	• Unmotivated repairmen • Poor training, tools • Parts non-availability	• Job redesign; reengineering the repair process • Built-in diagnostics • Reliability improvement, reducing necessity for spare parts
Customer misuse	Instruction not read or followed	Warranty labels; fail-safe designs
Customer non-comprehension	Non-user friendly features	Ergonomics, training
Late delivery	Poor forecasts; master schedules; MRPII; equipment breakdowns; supplier delinquency	Pull systems; just-in-time (JIT); total productive maintenance (TPM); small lots; reduced set-up times; supply management
Disconnected distributors/dealers	Limited loyalty to company	Distribution/dealer/customer councils
Order processing, billing, accounts receivables errors	Order inaccuracies, back orders, poor order tracking, routing errors, returns processing	Flow charting; next operation as customer; business process reengineering
Customer-contact employees not empowered	• Untrained, unmotivated, underpaid employees • Company rules and regulations as a straitjacket • Financial adjustments to customers unheard of	• Customer sensitivity training, "moments of truth" principles reinforced; more management attention (Hawthorne effect); pay incentives • De-emphasize all rules not affecting or adversely affecting the customer • Authorize employees (up to certain limits) to compensate angry, dissatisfied customers
Dictatorial management	Management by fear; micro-management	Management must change to leadership. Only the board of directors can effect the transition

baggage handling. Hotel executives, likewise, simulate a customer's encounters with the hotel, from the parking lot and the reception desk to the cashier and time of departure. The chairman of the renowned Marriott chain periodically becomes a bellman to learn of service to customers first-hand.

From Freephone Numbers to Ombudsman to Chief Customer Officer (CCO)

Another way companies facilitate linking up with customers is through the use of freephone numbers, where customers can call in with their inquiries, concerns and complaints. To demonstrate their commitment to customers, senior managers in a few enterprising companies answer these freephone lines one day in a month. They receive unfiltered feedback directly from customers, instead of the watered-down version fed to them by subordinates.

Some companies go further in appointing a senior executive as ombudsman (Swedish for "fixer") to provide a master information center for customers who might otherwise get lost in a corporate maze. The ultimate is the appointment of a top management person as the company's Chief Customer Officer (CCO) to be the customer's advocate in the entire corporation and to act as its "customer conscience." The CCO should be second in importance only to the CEO. He or she should marshal the company's entire customer activities, similar to a Chief Financial Officer (CFO) covering all its financial matters.

Statistics and Lies

There are good statistics and bad statistics. Many companies, enamored of this discipline, use it indiscriminately. Employing the seven tools of quality control, widely practiced by the Japanese, is an example of poor statistical tools for the wrong application. These tools, including plan, do, study, act (PDSA), Pareto charts, cause-and-effect diagrams, frequency distributions and control charts, are elementary and inadequate for problem solving in production. They are even worse in business practices or in dealing with customers.

Design of experiments (DOE), on the other hand, is a powerful tool for preventing and solving product and process problems; and is increasingly being used for analyzing and improving customer performance. Among the variants of this technique are the following:

- *Multivariate techniques* are used to stratify families of variation in dealing with customers, such as geographic locations; product or service complexity; volume; complaint categories; salesforce competency; time spent with customer etc.

- *Paired comparisons* are used to ferret out repetitive differences in a number of characteristics associated with good customers and complaining customers.

- Multiple regression analysis is used to separate strong and weak correlations between services or features offered and their perceived utility to customers.

Creative Stimuli

Other tools are also used to improve customer performance:

- *Brainstorming* is a well-known technique, frequently used by customer improvement teams. It is based on the premise of the worth of the final ideas for improvement being directly proportional to the number of ideas in an initial brainstorming session.

- *Force field analysis* arrays a set of driving forces necessary for improving a parameter (say, customer satisfaction) against a set of restraining forces constraining improvement. It then systematically plans measures to enhance the driving forces and simultaneously attenuate the restraining forces to achieve a much improved level of performance.

- *Value engineering* is a powerful discipline for improving the quality of a product, service or business process while simultaneously reducing its cost. Applied to any process or service that affects customers, it asks:

  – What does it do? (What is the function of the process?)

  – What does it cost?

  – What else can perform the function (with improved performance)?

  – What will that cost (at lower cost)?

  The improved process is generally a radical departure from the current one. Another facet of value engineering is asking the "5 Whys:"

  – Why do we need this process or method?

  – If the answer to the first question is "because...", you ask the second "why." To that answer, you ask the third "why" and so on until the process is either eliminated altogether, minified or modified for greater customer acceptance and lower cost.

Business Process Reengineering (BPR)

The ultimate application of business process reengineering (BPR) is to revolutionize the entire company — its organization structure; its methods of hiring, evaluating, compensating and promoting its employees; its very values and culture. Among several companies professing to have adopted BPR, hardly any have gone the full distance.

Nevertheless, companies can adopt a few BPR techniques through evolution rather than undertaking a full-blown revolution:

- *Cross-functional teams* can be utilized to convert a bureaucratic, vertical organization into a hard-hitting horizontal, interdisciplinary team to improve business processes and focus on customers.

- *Flow charting.* The cross-functional teams use flow charting (otherwise known as process mapping) to map every step in the business process, starting with the customer and going back to the start of the process. The cycle time (actual clock time) of each step as well as the total cycle time of the entire process are determined. Each step is then examined to see if it really adds value, especially from the customer's viewpoint. All non-value-added steps and their cycle times are eliminated or drastically reduced. Typically, flow charting can eliminate over two-thirds of the steps in such a process and half the total cycle time. The result is faster, higher-quality and lower-cost service to the customer.

- *"Out-of-box" thinking.* Flow charting is evolutionary — a starting point for improved service to the customer. It establishes only a basecamp in the climb to the top of the mountain. To get to the peak of maximum effectiveness, the entire process, flow chart and all, must be jettisoned using "out-of-box" thinking. This means developing radically new and creative ways to achieve process goals.

Customer-Contact Employees

Japanese CEOs frequently claim their primary task is the "caring and feeding of their young," i.e. their newer employees. In the service sector, where employees come into frequent contact with customers, top management must also nurture their employees. In the popular reverse pyramid organization structure, customer-contact employees are at the top of the pyramid — next only to the external customers. They must be empowered, using the following measures:

- Selection/hiring should be based on sensitivity to customers and team player and innovative potential. They should not be picked off the streets and hired as a "pair of hands."

- Compensation should be commensurate with the importance of interface with customers.

- Training can never be overemphasized. It should deal not only with a thorough knowledge of products and services, but also with skills in listening, innovation and defusing customer frustration and anger.

- Decision making should include the ability to change rules and regulations from those serving the company to those serving the customer and capture their satisfaction and loyalty.

- Morale should continually be assessed through management and customer surveys.

- Recognition by management for outstanding service to customers should become a way of life. It should include bonuses and other rewards, along with celebrations for the entire team.

THE CUSTOMER LOYALTY AUDIT

STEP 7: CONTINUOUS IMPROVEMENT

		RATING 1 2 3 4 5
A.	Corrective Actions on Typical Customer Complaints	
1.	The causes of the following typical customer complaints are identified and the appropriate corrective action tools utilized:	
	(a) product quality	
	(b) product reliability	
	(c) product liability	
	(d) field repair	
	(e) customer misuse	
	(f) customer non-comprehension	
	(g) delivery	
	(h) distributors/dealers	
	(i) customer services	
	(j) customer-contact employees	
	(k) management.	
2.	Top management regularly conducts audits on services rendered to customers.	
3.	800 numbers are made available to customers for contact with company officials	
4.	The company appoints an ombudsman, or preferably a Chief Customer Officer (CCO), to act as the customers' advocate within the company.	
5.	The company utilizes design of experiments to analyze and improve customer performance.	
6.	The company utilizes creative tools such as force field analysis and value engineering to improve customer performance.	
7.	The customer utilizes business process improvement, flow charting and "out-of-box" thinking to improve service to customers.	
8.	The company empowers its customer-contact employees to service its customers better.	

CONCLUSION

This briefing has advocated the need for a company to go beyond mere customer satisfaction to customer loyalty; to go beyond just market share, quantity of performance, to customer retention, quality of performance; to go beyond today's customers to customers for life. It has presented a roadmap for achieving customer loyalty. And it has lit the way with a self-assessment a company can employ to determine how far it has already gone on the road to customer loyalty and how much further it has to travel.

The results of long-term commitment to customer loyalty are captured in Table 4.[37]

TABLE 4		
PARAMETER	CUSTOMER-FOCUSED COMPANIES	AVERAGE COMPANY
Return on equity	17%	11%
Profit on sales	9.2%	5%
Market share growth	6%	2%
Cost reduction	10–15%	2–3%
Stock price growth	16.9%	10.9%

The bottom line is: customer loyalty pays and pays handsomely.

REFERENCES

1. Goodman and Malech, "Issues in the Development of Valid, Actionable Satisfaction Measurement and Incentive Systems."

2. REL Consultancy Group, "1994 Survey of Customer Retention and Corporate Profitability."

3. Robert D. Buzzell and Bradley T. Gale (1987) *The PIMS Principle,* New York: Free Press.

4. J. K. Cannie and D. Chapman (1991) *Keep Customers for Life,* Amacom.

5. Keki R. Bhote (1991) "The Next Operations As Customer," American Management Association.

6. A.T. Kearney (1994) *The Customer Satisfaction Audit*, Zurich: Strategic Direction.

7. Nancy Gibbs (1995) "The E. Q. Factor," *Time,* Oct. 2.

8. REL Consultancy Group, "1994 Survey of Customer Retention and Corporate Profitability."

9. Thomas J. Peters and Robert H. Waterman (1982) *In Search of Excellence,* Harper & Row.

10. Keki R. Bhote (1989) "Strategic Supply Management," American Management Association.

11. Dawn Iacobucci, Kent Grayson & Amy Ostrom (1994) "Customer Satisfaction Fables," *Sloan Management Review*, Summer.

12. Keki R. Bhote (1994) "Boss Performance Appraisal: A Metric Whose Time Has Gone," *Employment Relations Today*, Spring.

13. Robert W. Galvin (1991) "Idea of Ideas," Motorola University Press.

14. Keki R. Bhote (1992) "Powerful Quality Tools for the 21st Century," International Quality Symposium, Milan, Italy, September.

15. Keki R. Bhote (1994) "Boss Performance Appraisal: A Metric Whose Time Has Gone," *Employment Relations Today*, Spring.

16. J. K. Cannie and D. Chapman (1991) *Keep Customers for Life,* Amacom.

17. Keki R. Bhote (1991) "World Class Quality — Using Design of Experiments to Make It Happen," American Management Association.

18. Keki R. Bhote (1989) "Strategic Supply Management," American Management Association.

19. Larry Miles (1982) *Value Analysis Techniques*, McGraw Hill.

20. Michael Spendolini (1994) "Benchmarking," American Management Association.

21. Keki R. Bhote (1991) "World Class Quality — Using Design of Experiments to Make It Happen," American Management Association.

22. Keki R. Bhote (1989) "Strategic Supply Management," American Management Association.

23. Jeffrey Boothroyd & Peter Dewhurst (1987) *Product Design for Manufacturing & Assembly*, Boothroyd & Dewhurst, Inc.

24. Keki R. Bhote (1989) "Strategic Supply Management," American Management Association.

25. Keki R. Bhote (1989) "Strategic Supply Management," American Management Association.

26. Larry Miles (1982) *Value Analysis Techniques*, McGraw Hill.

27. Shigeo Shingo, *Zero Q. C. Source Inspection and Poka Yoke*, Productivity Press.

28. J. K. Cannie and D. Chapman (1991) *Keep Customers for Life*, Amacom.

29. Keki R. Bhote (1989) "Strategic Supply Management," American Management Association.

30. Kcki R. Bhote (1989) "Strategic Supply Management," American Management Association.

31. Keki R. Bhote (1991) "The Next Operations As Customer," American Management Association.

32. Keki R. Bhote (1989) "Strategic Supply Management," American Management Association.

33. Keki R. Bhote (1989) "Strategic Supply Management," American Management Association.

34. Yoji Akao (1988) *Quality Function Deployment*, Productivity Press.

35. *The Benchmarking Portfolio*, Zurich: Strategic Direction.

36. John Goodman & Arlene Malech, "Issues in the Development of Valid, Actionable Satisfaction Measurement and Incentives Systems," TARP (Technical Assistance Research Program Institute) working paper.

37. A.T. Kearney (1994) *The Customer Satisfaction Audit*, Zurich: Strategic Direction.

Part 3

THE AUDIT PROCESS

This section addresses the logistical and process requirements of conducting an audit. The topics covered in this section include:

- Staffing the audit team

- Creating an audit project plan

- Laying the groundwork for the audit

- Analyzing audit results

- Sharing audit results

- Writing effective audit reports

- Dealing with resistance to audit recommendations

- Building an ongoing audit program

Staffing the Audit Team

Who conducts the audit is as important in many ways as how the audit is conducted. In fact, the people selected for the audit team will, in large part, determine how the audit is done, how results are analyzed, and how findings are reported. The following list includes general characteristics of effective audit teams for most areas:

- Consists of three to four people.

- Reports to CEO or other senior executive.

- Represents a carefully selected range of skills and experience.

More than four people may be needed for an audit team if data gathering is labor intensive, as when large numbers of customers or employees must be interviewed. However, audit teams of more than six or seven people present problems of maintaining uniformity and communicating audit progress and findings during the course of the evaluation.

Selecting an Audit Team Leader

The audit team leader will play a strong role in shaping both the data gathering and the findings from the audit. The strength of the team leader will also influence the acceptance of the audit, both in terms of enlisting cooperation in the data gathering phase and in securing support for improvement initiatives that grow out of the audit. Because of the importance of this role, care should be taken in selecting the appropriate person for the job. The following qualities are found in successful audit team leaders:

- Has a good relationship with the CEO or with the executive-level sponsor of the audit.

- Is well-liked and well-respected at all levels of the organization, especially in the area to be audited.

- Has good interpersonal skills; can maintain good relationships even in difficult circumstances.

- Has good analytical skills; can assimilate and process large amounts of complex data quickly.

- Has some knowledge of the function or area being audited.

- Has extensive knowledge of the type of process being audited.

- Communicates ideas clearly and effectively.

Skills to Be Represented on the Audit Team

Once the team leader has been chosen, audit team members should be selected on the basis of what each can bring to the project. Selection efforts should focus on developing a balanced representation of the following qualities:

- A variety of tenures in the organization, with relative newcomers preferably having experience in other organizations.

- A variety of familiarity with the area (function or site) being audited. Those who are intimately familiar with the area can serve as guides to the less familiar; those who are new to the area can provide objectivity and ask questions that might never be considered by those more involved in the area.

- Considerable familiarity with the type of process being audited. For this reason, many organizations call on people filling roles in similar processes from other parts of the company to work on audit teams.

- Good analytical skills.

- Good interpersonal skills.

- Good facilitation and interviewing skills.

- Good communication skills.

- An understanding of the company's strategy and direction.

CREATING AN AUDIT PROJECT PLAN

Creating an audit project plan accomplishes the following objectives:

- Ensures the allocation of adequate resources, or helps audit team members be prepared to improvise in the face of short resources.

- Ensures the audit is timed so resources are available that may be in high demand.

- Creates clear expectations in the minds of team members about what must be done, and when — especially important when they are not committed to the project full-time.

- Ensures accountability for what must be done, who is responsible for which tasks, and when the audit must be completed.

Financial audits often rely on the Critical Path Method (CPM) of project planning. This method was originally developed by the US Department of Defense during World War II to facilitate the timely completion of weapons development and production. It has since been modified to plan a wide variety of projects. The following outline is a simplification of CPM. It suggests the aspects of a project that should be taken into account during the planning phase.

Critical Path Method

In developing the project plan, audit team members should ask and answer the following questions:

- *What tasks must be performed?*

This list should include the major tasks outlined in the audits, along with subtasks that grow out of those major headings. It should also include any tasks mandated by unique circumstances in the company performing the self-assessment. The audit team may want to brainstorm about tasks that need to be performed, then refine the list to reflect the work priorities of the audit.

- *In what order will the tasks be completed?*

Answering this question should include an analysis of which tasks and sub tasks are dependent on others. Which tasks cannot begin until another has been completed? Which tasks can be done at any time? The audit team may want to place the ordered task on a time line, with start dates, expected duration of the step, and end dates outlined for each task.

- *Who will perform each task?*

Most tasks will be performed by members of the audit team. These assignments should be made by taking the strengths of each team member into consideration, as well as the time availability of each person. Equity of work load should also be taken into account. If tasks are to be assigned to people not on the audit team, those individuals should be included or consulted at this point.

- *What resources will be needed for each step?*

Each task should be analyzed in terms of the personnel, budget, equipment, facilities, support services, and any other resources that will be needed for its completion. The team should assess the availability of all of the resources. Consideration should be given to the task ordering completed earlier. Are some resources subject to competing demands, and therefore difficult to secure at a particular time? How far in advance do arrangements for resources need to be made? Does the task order or time line need to be revised in light of what is known about resource availability?

- *Where is the slack time?*

Slack time is unscheduled time between dependent tasks. Slack provides a degree of flexibility in altering the start dates of subsequent tasks. Slack time signals that a task has a range of possible start dates. It is used to determine the critical path.

- *What is the critical path?*

The critical path in a project is the set of tasks that must be completed in a sequential, chronological order. If any task on the critical path is not completed, all subsequent tasks will be delayed. Delays at any point in the critical path will result in an equivalent delay in the completion of the total project.

Regardless of the method used to develop the project plan, no project, regardless how simple, is ever completed in exact accordance with its plan. However, having a project plan allows the team to gauge its progress, anticipate problems and determine where alternative approaches are needed.

Laying the Groundwork for the Audit

Once the team has been selected and a project plan developed, the audit leader should prepare those who will be involved in and affected by the audit for the team's visit or for data-gathering. The following steps will help the audit to run more smoothly:

Communicate Executive Support for the Audit

Demonstrating executive support for the audit accomplishes two goals. First, it increases the chances that those involved in the area being audited will cooperate with data gathering efforts. Second, it shows executive support for the area being audited and suggests a commitment to improving the area's performance.

In many companies, the audit is introduced by the executive sponsor of the audit by means of a memo. The memo should explain the purpose of the audit and ask for the support of everyone in the area being audited. This memo is distributed to everyone within the company who will be affected by or involved in the data gathering process. The most effective memos explain how the audit results will be used, reassuring those who will be responding to audit team requests about the motives of the audit. The credibility of such memos is also bolstered when previous audits have been acted upon with positive results.

Make Arrangements with the Area to Be Audited

The audit team leader should check with the appropriate manager in charge of the process or site being audited to arrange for any required on-site visits, interviewing, surveys, focus groups, or written information needed for the audit. The team leader should also explain the purpose, scope, and expected duration of the audit; review the project plan with the manager; and answer any questions the manager has about the audit.

The team leader should also work with the appropriate manager or managers to determine how the audit can be conducted with the least impact on the flow of work. This may include discussions about the timing of the audit, the options for data gathering, the availability of needed data, and possibilities for generating the necessary information quickly and easily. Finding ways to make data collection more efficient and effective is especially important when the audit is part of an ongoing program, rather than an isolated assessment.

Develop a Protocol or Checklist

A protocol or checklist can be used by the audit team to outline the issues that are central to the audit. Written guides can help the leaders of those areas being audited to prepare for the audit. A protocol represents a plan of what the audit team will do to accomplish the objectives of the audit. It is an important tool of the audit, since it not only serves as the audit team's guide to collecting data, but also as a record of the audit procedures completed by the team. In some cases, audit teams may even want to format the checklist in a way that allows them to record their field notes directly on the checklist.

The checklist should include no more than twenty major items, and checklists should be updated with each audit in order to ensure that the appropriate measures are taken. Items where improvement initiatives have been successful should be eliminated from the checklist, with newly identified possibilities for improvement opportunities added.

ANALYZING AUDIT RESULTS

Discovering gaps between a company's targets and its actual performance is a relatively easy task. Tools are provided to assist audit teams in assessing their performance in a given area. In most cases, more opportunities for improvement will be uncovered by an audit than can be addressed by the resources and energy available. Therefore, one of the most difficult aspects of analyzing the results of an audit lies in determining which opportunities are the most important for managers to pursue.

Because resources and energy for pursuing improvement initiatives are limited, choices must be made about which options are most important. Sometimes these decisions are based on political winds in the company, or on what has worked well in the past, or on personal preferences of top management. However, scarce resources will be used more effectively if allocated to the areas where they will have the greatest impact. Managers must also determine the most effective way to approach initiatives. This section discusses criteria for prioritizing opportunities that grow out of audit findings.

The Novations Strategic Alignment Model

The mid-1980s saw the birth of the "excellence" movement, where many companies tried to achieve excellence in every area of endeavour. Although the movement created an awareness of the need for management improvements, it failed to consider that not all management processes are equal in terms of producing benefits. As a result, leading organizations in today's environment focus on performing well in a few core areas. Knowing what those core areas are depends on a clear vision of the company's strategy.

Strategic thinking about which areas should be improved involves much more than taking an inventory of current capabilities and weaknesses. If it did not, existing capabilities would always determine strategic objectives, and organizational growth and development would come to a halt. To set priorities strategically, companies must decide which improvement opportunities fall in the following categories:

- What to do themselves.

- What to do with someone else.

- What to contract others to do.

- What not to do.

THE CUSTOMER LOYALTY AUDIT

**FIGURE 1
CATEGORIES OF WORK**

All work activities
- Unit of Competitive Advantage Work
- Value-Added Support Work
- Essential Support Work
- Non-Essential Work (crossed out)

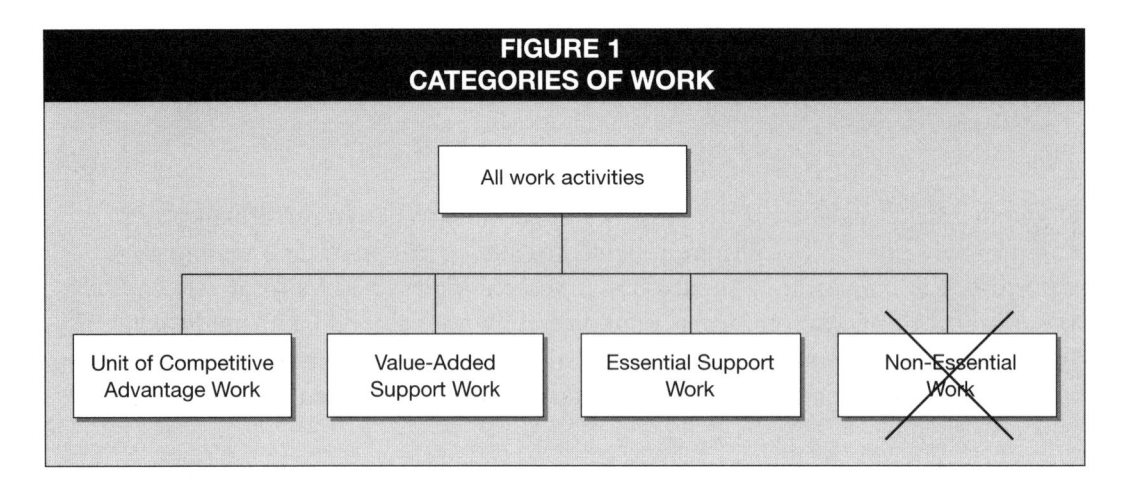

Figure 1 illustrates the four categories of work.

Unit of Competitive Advantage (UCA) Work includes work and capabilities that create distinctiveness for the business in the marketplace.

Value-added Support Work facilitates the accomplishment of the UCA work. For example, a company may have a technology orientation rather than a service orientation, but an effective logistics process may help them to improve their UCA work of providing cutting edge technology.

Essential Support Work neither creates advantage nor facilitates the work that creates advantage, but must be done if businesses are to continue to operate (includes such things as paying taxes, maintaining payroll records, etc.).

Nonessential Work is activity that has lost its usefulness but continues to be done because of tradition.

Despite their sophistication in dealing with other aspects of business, most managers have archaic views of the different types of work. Many of their models for characterizing work have come from a finance or accounting orientation. Accounting terms such as overhead, direct labor, and indirect labor may be useful as a way to report costs, but they provide little understanding about the relative strategic importance of the work. Yet these classifications are frequently used to determine how work is organized and where resources are allocated.

The concept of unit of competitive advantage (UCA) helps to explain why some organizations either emphasize the wrong capabilities or de-emphasize the right capabilities. UCA also explains why some forms of improvement lead to competitive disadvantage, and why some businesses consistently outperform their competitors by gaining greater leverage from their competitive advantages.

A company's UCA includes the critical processes that create distinctiveness within an established strategic direction. It is based on the premise that businesses create competitive advantage when they focus their attention on a few key processes and implement those key processes in world-class fashion. For example, continuous improvement is a popular management program that assumes benefit from any kind of ongoing improvement. Generally speaking, however, continuous improvement program will only create competitive advantage when an organization defines a strategic direction, clarifies strategic objectives, and determines its UCA. These crucial prerequisites tell where continuous improvement efforts should be focused to create maximum leverage. They suggest what kinds of work to improve interdependently, what kinds to improve separately, and what kinds not to waste time on. They even signal when continuous improvement is more likely to create competitive disadvantage rather than competitive advantage.

UCA Initiatives Should Take Priority

Understanding what work falls under which categories requires a clear understanding of the company's strategy. The initiatives resulting from an audit that affect the Unit of Competitive Advantage work processes should clearly have the highest priority among improvement projects. Value-added support initiatives should be second priority, and essential support work should be the third priority. Nonessential work should not be continued.

Once improvement opportunities that will have the greatest impact on the achievement of the company's goals have been identified, the following ideas can be used to lend further insight into how opportunities identified through an audit should be prioritized:

- *Focus on the two or three most important areas.*

Insisting that action be taken on all of the problems uncovered by the audit may overwhelm the people who are responsible for bringing about those changes. Flatter organizations and leaner work forces mean that people are already being asked to do more work with fewer resources and less time. Producing a long list of improvement initiatives may prompt people to dismiss all of them because they don't have time to complete the whole list.

- *Focus on the areas that can be changed.*

Emphasizing problems that are beyond the control of the people who are responsible to work on process improvement only leads to cynicism and a sense of powerlessness. By focusing on things that are within the sphere of influence, accountability for each part of the action plan can be clearly defined.

- *Include as priorities some improvements that can be made quickly.*

Rapid, visible improvement helps build support for more complicated initiatives. Quick improvements also reassure people of management's support for long-term improvement. Seeing immediate improvement helps to build commitment at all levels to the process, and helps build momentum for further change.

- *Emphasize the improvements that seem essential to long-term success.*

Essential improvements may involve sensitive issues or difficult problems, such as deficiencies in fundamental skill levels within the organization or basic strategy issues. These problems are not only difficult and expensive to address, but may also cause a great deal of personal pain or require significant individual adjustment. Nevertheless, long-term improvement requires a commitment to dealing with difficult issues rather than avoiding them.

Sharing Audit Results

In most cases, audit results will be presented to various interested people in a feedback meeting. Those in attendance may include members of the executive team, managers who work in the area covered by the audit, the audit team members, and anyone else who is affected by or interested in the results. The meeting should be conducted by members of the audit team. The purpose is to present their findings, and make recommendations for capitalizing on opportunities for improvement.

Conducting Effective Feedback Meetings

The audit team's strategy for the meeting should be to present a clear and simple picture of the current situation as revealed by the audit. This may be a moment of truth for those who have been anticipating the audit results. The feedback meeting for an audit holds both excitement and anxiety: excitement that the future will be bright, and anxiety that shortcomings in individual performance will be highlighted and demands made for personal change. As a result, the meeting must be carefully managed in order to lead to productive change. The following structure is one recommended format for conducting a feedback meeting.

- *Introduce the meeting and preview its agenda.*

This might include an overview of the original intent of the audit, introduction of the audit team, and a brief summary of the meeting's agenda. This step should take no more than five minutes.

- *Present the audit findings.*

Audit findings should summarize the most important points revealed by the data gathered in the audit process. They should be presented separately from the audit recommendations in order to allow people to digest the two parts of the presentation separately. Clearing up misunderstandings about the findings may make the group more accepting of the team's recommendations.

The presentation of the audit findings should take comparatively little time. Audits almost always generate much more data than can be effectively presented or digested in a feedback meeting. The goal of the audit team should be to zero in on the two or three most important points learned from the audit, and present enough supporting data to illustrate those points.

Presenting too much data about audit findings has a number of negative effects. It encourages people to conduct their own analysis of the audit data. To a certain extent, this is a healthy and normal reaction. If others understand the evidence that supports the conclusions drawn by the audit team, they are more likely to accept and own the audit results. Therefore, they will be more committed to the changes brought about by the audit results. However, when people immerse themselves in large amounts of data, they may become victims of "analysis paralysis": they may spend unnecessary time attempting to explain contradictory data, or trying to understand methods used by others to gather data.

- *Present audit recommendations.*

Presenting the audit recommendations should be the central point of the meeting. The recommendations should grow out of the data highlights presented. The audit team should view the recommendations as discussion points for the meeting, rather than as absolute action items.

A common mistake in feedback meetings is to spend most of the meeting on presenting data and recommendations. It is easy for audit team members to become enamored of data they have invested considerable time and energy to collect and analyze. Others in the audience will probably also be interested in the details of the data collected. However, if too much time is spent on discussing the recommendations, the meeting will end before a commitment to action has been made.

- *Ask others to react to the data.*

The reactions of top management and those responsible for implementing audit recommendations will determine the ultimate value of the audit data. Therefore, the feedback meeting is a good time to resolve questions or problems with the findings and recommendations as they have been presented. If resistance to the audit findings is not resolved in the feedback meeting, opportunities for improvement may be lost.

Those attending the meeting may offer their opinions willingly. If not, the audit team members should ask the others in the room for their reaction to what has been presented.

- *Develop preliminary action plans.*

The detailed action plans should grow out of the recommendations made by the audit team. They should specifically address the question of who should do what by when. Formal accountability mechanisms should be established before the end of the meeting, such as the scheduling of subsequent meetings or follow-up check points.

Writing Effective Audit Reports

There are three fundamental purposes for writing a formal report at the conclusion of an audit:

- An audit report may be a stand-alone summary of the audit. This approach is not recommended, inasmuch as the report is likely to be filed away, making the probability of action unlikely.

- The report may supplement a feedback meeting, providing those in attendance with documentation and an outline to follow.

- The report should also serve as a baseline document to make measurement of performance improvement possible in future audits.

Because the written report is the most enduring part of the audit presentation, it should be well written and easy to understand. The following tips will lead to the preparation of effective written audit reports.

Focus on a Few Key Points

The audit presentation should focus on the two or three most important findings. It is impossible to present all of the data gathered in the audit to those who were not on the audit team. It is also not advisable to present every detail of the data. The audit team members should trust their own judgment about what the highlights of the study were, and present enough data to support that judgment. For each of the major findings, the team may want to include the following information:

- What is the problem?

- Why does it exist?

- What happens if the problem is not fixed:

  — in the short term?

  — in the long term?

- Recommend solutions.

- Outline expected benefits.

THE CUSTOMER LOYALTY AUDIT

Prepare an Outline Before Writing the First Draft

A good outline ensures that the logic of the report is clear, and that ideas proceed in an order that makes sense. The following outline provides one approach that works effectively.

Background

This section should establish the framework for the audit in terms of:

- Providing a brief discussion of the overall purpose of the audit.

- Identifying the role of the audit team in the overall process.

- Establishing the limitations of the audit methodology to ensure that others utilize the results provided in the report appropriately.

Objectives

This section should identify specific objectives of the audit in terms of types of information the team was expected to generate.

Methodology

The methodology section should describe the mechanics of the audit and include the following information:

- Types of assessment used (survey, interviews, focus groups, etc.).

- Data sources, or the sample groups for each of the types of assessment used.

- Time frame during which the audit was conducted.

- Other pertinent details about how the audit was conducted.

Findings

This section is designed to provide others with a review of the "facts" that came out of the audit. Except in cases where an audit checks regulatory compliance, only the most significant findings should be discussed in any detail in the report. This section should also include briefly presented data supporting the findings.

Conclusions

This section should report the audit team's interpretation of what the facts of the audit mean in light of the objectives stated at the outset of the audit.

Recommendations

This section includes suggestions from the audit team on how to close the performance gaps identified in the audit. The degree of specificity to be included in the audit report will vary from company to company and audit to audit.

Appendix

This portion of the formal report should include any of the following items that are relevant to the audit:

- A copy of any questionnaires or survey instruments used in the audit.

- A summary of the data gathered in the course of the audit.

- Recommendations for subsequent audits based on the team's experience.

Present Audit Findings Accurately

Those who read the report will no doubt be somewhat familiar with the area covered by the audit. They may notice discrepancies between what they know about the subject and what is reported in the written document. Spotting one inaccuracy may lead the readers to discredit all of the findings, conclusions and recommendations. Audit team members should be careful to report data as it was actually generated, and to describe the impact of the findings accurately.

Use Clear, Concise Language

Every statement included in the report should be based on sound evidence developed or reviewed during the audit. Whatever is said must be supported or supportable. Speculation should be avoided. Generalities and vague reporting will only confuse and mislead those that the report should influence or inform. For example, a report using the terms some, a few, or not all can leave the reader confused about the significance of the finding. Specific quantities should be used, such as, "of the ten samples taken, two were found to be…", "Three of five respondents said that…", and so on. Statements should be qualified as needed, and any unconfirmed data or information should be identified as such.

Ideas or sentences that do not amplify the central theme should be eliminated. The report should not identify individuals or highlight the mistakes of individuals.

Use Good Grammar and Style

Basic grammar and style rules should be followed in writing the text. Below are some examples:

- Avoid extreme terms, such as alarming, deplorable, gross negligence, etc.

- Avoid using redundant or lengthy phrases, such as calling something an emergency situation when the word emergency alone will do.

- Avoid verbs camouflaged as nouns or adjectives. For example, use "the new procedure will reduce error entries," rather than "The new procedure will accomplish a reduction of error entries."

- Avoid indirect expressions where possible. For example, "Many instances of poor management were found," is more direct than saying, "There were many instances of poor judgment found."

- Use short, familiar words. Use words that are easily understandable to everyone and that convey the message concisely.

- Keep sentences short. Most writing experts suggest that an average sentence should be between 15 and 18 words. Packing too many ideas into a single sentence confuses and tires readers.

The audit team should provide enough background information in the report so that the reader clearly understands who conducted the audit and what the audit did or did not include. The purpose of the report as well as the purpose and scope of the audit should also be described in a manner that enables the reader to know why the report was written and who should take corrective action.

Timing of the Report

The timing of audit reports is critical to the overall reporting process and must be carefully thought out. In many cases, a written draft of the audit report is prepared one to three weeks before the feedback meeting. This draft then goes through a review and another report is prepared in time for the team's presentation. A final report may be completed after the feedback session has been held in order to record changes resulting from that meeting.

Dealing with Resistance to Recommendations

Most audit teams feel that if they can present their ideas clearly and logically, and have the best interests of the company or department at heart, managers will accept the recommendations made as part of the audit and follow the team's recommendations. Many people who have worked in organizations, however, find that no matter how reasonably recommendations are presented, they are all too often not implemented.

Implementation usually fails because it requires people to change their ways of working. That change requires a great deal of effort, energy, and risk; therefore, change is usually resisted. Resistance is an emotional process; people may embrace recommendations based on their logic, but fail to implement them because of the emotional resistance to the personal change involved. Resistance is a predictable, natural, and necessary part of the learning process. Although resistance may cause audit team members to feel they have missed the mark in terms of the recommendations they have made, it actually often signals accuracy in having interpreted the organization's needs. By dealing with the resistance directly, audit teams can work through barriers to implementing process improvements.

What Are the Signs of Resistance?

In many cases, resistance may be expressed directly. Direct objections to recommendations are relatively easy to address, inasmuch as they can be discussed and resolved. When recommendations are being presented, team members should stop frequently to allow those who are listening to the report to voice any objections or disagreements. Those who are presenting the data should be careful not to become defensive or to punish those who express reservations about the recommendations. It is impossible to deal with objections unless they are voiced; therefore, the audit team should welcome the expression of objections or differences of opinion. The following tips may be used for surfacing and dealing with direct resistance:

- Provide many opportunities for others to express their concerns.

- Carefully clarify any confusing concerns.

- Deal with important or easy concerns immediately. Defer the remainder.

- Summarize the concerns before moving on. Show that concerns have been heard.

- It may even be helpful to list concerns on a flip chart or blackboard.

If direct resistance continues, the following steps may be necessary:

- Talk about the differences of opinion.

- Voice concern and support for negotiating a resolution.

- Avoid struggles for control of the situation.

Dealing with Indirect Resistance

In other cases, resistance may be subtle and elusive. Indirect resistance is difficult to identify and deal with because its manifestations seem logical. People who are experiencing indirect resistance may feel that they are "getting the run around." Many different forms of resistance may manifest themselves in a single meeting:

- Request for more detail.

- Providing too much detail in response to questions.

- Complaining that there isn't enough time to implement recommendations.

- Claiming that the recommendations are impractical.

- Attacking those who propose improvement initiatives.

- Acting confused.

- Responding with silence.

- Intellectualizing about the data.

- Moralizing that problems wouldn't exist if it weren't for "those people".

- Agreeing to implement recommendations with no intention of acting on them.

- Asking questions about methodology.

- Arguing that previous problems have resolved themselves.

- Focusing on solutions before findings are fully understood.

Almost any of these responses is legitimate in moderate amounts. For example, members of the group may have concerns about the audit's methodology that should be considered. Managers may realistically wonder where they will find the time to implement recommendations. However, if refusal to act on recommendations persists once legitimate concerns have been addressed, then the audit team is probably facing indirect resistance.

Many models used in sales training provide recommendations for overcoming resistance. These methods suggest the use of data and logical arguments to win the point and convince the other person to buy whatever is being sold. These models work well for direct resistance. However, indirect resistance is normally based on feelings rather than logic. Therefore, the only way to truly overcome resistance is to deal with the emotional processes that cause it to happen in the first place. It is almost impossible to talk people out of the way they feel.

Feelings pass and change when they are expressed directly. A key skill for audit teams that are attempting to implement recommendations is to ask the people who are presenting resistance to put directly into words what they are experiencing. The most effective way to make this happen is for the audit team members to address directly what is happening in the situation. The following keys provide help in surfacing and dealing with indirect resistance.

- *Work once or twice with the person's concern, even when it feels as if he or she is resisting recommendations.*

By attempting to work with the problem stated by the person raising a concern, audit team members can determine whether the concern is legitimate or whether it is an excuse for not taking action. If the issues raised are legitimate, the person should show some willingness to discuss and resolve them. If the issues are manifestations of indirect resistance, the person will probably respond with other forms of resistance.

- *Identify the form the resistance is taking.*

Paying attention to the dynamics of a discussion can provide important clues as to whether or not a person is resisting recommendations. If a person is consistently distancing him or herself from those who are presenting the audit findings, using gestures or postures that suggest tension or discomfort, while at the same time presenting arguments for why the recommendations presented are inappropriate, it is probably a sign of resistance. The non-verbal responses of the presenters may also signal the onset of resistance. If presenters feel that they are suppressing negative feelings or becoming bored or irritated, it may be further evidence that the client is resisting.

Once presenters become aware of the resistance, the next step is to put it into words. This is best done by using neutral, everyday language. The skill is to describe the form of the resistance in a way that encourages the person to make a more direct statement of the reservation he or she is experiencing.

One general rule for stating what type of resistance is being manifested is to phrase the statement in common, non-threatening language. Statements should be made in the same tone and language that would be used to address a problem with a spouse or close friend. The statement should be made with as little evaluation as possible; it is the presenter's observation about what is happening in the situation.

A second general rule for surfacing indirect resistance involves not talking for a couple of moments after the presenter has stated what he or she has observed. There may be a temptation to elaborate on the observation, or to support it with evidence. However, continuing the statement will reduce the tension in the situation. Without tension, the person who is resisting feels no discomfort, and is unlikely to address the issue directly. Moreover, elaborating on the original statement may increase the other person's defensiveness and reduce the chances of solving the problem.

If stating the problem in direct, non-punishing terms fails to bring the resistance out into the open, there may be little more the audit team can do to overcome the indirect resistance. The best strategy in this case is to avoid resisting the resistance. Team members should support the person who is resisting and proceed with the implementation of recommendations to the extent possible.

Building an Ongoing Audit Program

As the pace of change increases, and as organization leaders become more and more committed to continuously improving their effectiveness and efficiency, audits of all types of processes will become more common. The most effective companies will establish program of ongoing audits, whereby a number of goals can be accomplished:

- Performance improvements can be measured over time.

- Important changes in the company's environment can be systematically monitored.

- Managers can make a habit of change and improvement, rather than resisting it.

- Those areas that are of highest importance to the company can be routinely improved.

- Processes can be modified to be in alignment with changes in strategy or in the environment.

As with all management techniques, however, an enduring program of ongoing audits requires that audits become integrated into the overall management system. The following guidelines are keys to weaving audits into the fabric of day-to-day operations.

Establish Support for Ongoing Audits

While support for audits begins at the executive level, ownership for the audit process must be felt throughout the organization if an ongoing program is to be successful. The following actions will help to broaden support for the audit process, while ensuring greater benefit from the audit.

- *Share the results of the audit with everyone throughout the organization.*

By keeping others informed about the results of an audit, managers reassure those who participate in and are affected by the audit of the integrity of the process. Employees sometimes become suspicious of probing investigators; they may have doubts about how the information will be used, or whether the information will be used. By sharing audit results, managers make an implicit commitment to improving the processes that have been evaluated.

- *Act on the audit results.*

Questions will be raised about continuing audits if early assessments bear no fruits. Failing to act on performance gaps that are identified leads to cynicism and lack of trust among those who work with the problems daily. On the other hand, improving a process can create the momentum that comes from accomplishment. Committing resources and attention to the improvement opportunities revealed by an audit also shows management commitment to the improvement process.

- *Let others know when performance has improved.*

Communicating the positive results from an audit is one way of rewarding the people who contributed to that improvement. It also builds faith in the effectiveness of the audit process. Moreover, showing that performance has improved is another means of reassuring people of a commitment to the improvement process.

- *Reward people for their part in improvements.*

Increasing efficiency and effectiveness can often be a threatening experience for those who are involved in a work process. Improving the way resources are used often means eliminating the need for some of the people who have been involved in the process. Although flatter, leaner organizations often preclude the possibility of offering promotions, managers should nevertheless attempt to ensure that people who contribute to performance improvement find their own situations better rather than worse as a result.

Rewards for helping to close performance gaps may span a range from thanking people for their efforts to planning a group celebration to offering bonuses or pay increases for improvement. Rewards are especially meaningful when people are allowed to suggest what rewards they would like for their contribution. This may provide managers with new ideas for rewards that may be less costly to the organization than financial recognition.

- *Involve a wide variety of people in the audit process.*

People can be involved in the audit process in many ways. By involving people from a broad spectrum, more people learn about audit techniques and results, thus spreading commitment to the audit process throughout the organization. By involving many people in the data-gathering process, employees feel that action plans growing out of the audit were a result of their input. Excluding people from the data-gathering phase usually reduces the feeling of ownership for the results, thus making people feel as if initiatives are being imposed on them. By the same token, involving a broad range of people in the development of action plans expands ownership for the plans and allows for the generation of more ideas.

Part 4

IMPLEMENTING A CUSTOMER LOYALTY AUDIT: QUESTIONS AND CHECKLISTS

This part of the Customer Loyalty Audit comprises a series of questions based on the seven steps in *Part 2: A Seven-Step Audit for Attaining and Maintaining Customer Loyalty*. All of these questions have been designed to help you plan and implement your audit in a straightforward and practical manner, covering the relevant parts of the audit in the correct sequence.

- Step 1 Top Management Commitment and Involvement
- Step 2 Internal Benchmarking — Establishing a Baseline
- Step 3 Determining Customer Requirement
- Step 4 Assessing the Capabilities of Competition
- Step 5 Measuring Customer Satisfaction and Customer Loyalty
- Step 6 Analyzing Customer and Competitive Feedback
- Step 7 Continuous Improvement

Note: Before you answer the questions that have been listed throughout this part of the audit, you might like to refer to *Part 1: Transition from Customer Satisfaction to Customer Loyalty*, which has the following sections:

- What Will You Get from this Audit?
- Customer Satisfaction — Necessary But Not Sufficient
- Customer Loyalty: the Ultimate Challenge
- Customer Differentiation: Focus on "Core" Customers
- The Ten Inviolate Principles of Customer Loyalty.

Additionally, useful background information is given for each step before the questions themselves are listed.

This audit lists several success factors contributing to the effectiveness of each step. Each success factor should be given a rating of 1 to 5 by the self-assessment team, with 1 being the worst and 5 being the best. The criteria are listed in the main text of Step 2, Part 2: *A Seven-Step Audit for Attaining and Maintaining Customer Loyalty*.

Step 1

TOP MANAGEMENT COMMITMENT AND INVOLVEMENT

BACKGROUND INFORMATION

In this first step of the audit, the three steps that follow will be examined.

1. Values — not a NATO game.

2. Demonstrating customer commitment to employees.

3. Customer loyalty audit and scoring systems.

Answering the questions below will help you to deal with these areas in turn.

QUESTIONS

1. Values — Not a NATO Game

- Is it understood that for values to have true value, they must be:
  - ❏ lived and breathed by top management
  - ❏ disseminated to all employees
  - ❏ studied by them
  - ❏ accepted by them?

- Will top managers model the behavior they want in order to gain employee acceptance?

Note: A behavior followed by a reward is a positive reinforcement and likely to be repeated; a behavior followed by punishment is a strong deterrent and not likely to be repeated.

2. Demonstrating Customer Commitment to Employees

- In order to pursue customer satisfaction and loyalty, do top management:
  - ❏ pay attention to the metrics associated with customer satisfaction and especially customer loyalty
  - ❏ have uncompromising integrity in dealing with customers and the public
  - ❏ have trust in employees and their ability to grow as a reflection of trust in customers

THE CUSTOMER LOYALTY AUDIT

- ❏ use strong and urgent corrective action on the element of customer satisfaction missing from the company's product
- ❏ personally spend time with customers
- ❏ commit time, personal attention and money
- ❏ give customer-contact employees authorization to make their own decisions in dealing with customers — especially irate ones — even if it costs the company to do so
- ❏ reward those employees who provide excellent customer service and celebrate such achievers
- ❏ communicate the commitment to the customer in publications, advertisements, newsletters, news releases to the media and annual reports
- ❏ encourage feedback from employees, publicising and rewarding their ideas
- ❏ establish customer satisfaction and loyalty as a key part of the agenda at periodic meetings?

3. Customer Loyalty Audit and Scoring System

Note: Each step of the process for attaining and retaining customer loyalty contains a self-assessment audit to measure its effectiveness.

- Will the self-assessment audit be undertaken by a cross-function team?

- Will this team consist of a member from:
  - ❏ top management (preferably the Chief Customer Officer (CCO))
  - ❏ sales/marketing
  - ❏ service
  - ❏ quality assurance?

- Will it, especially, have a representative from customer-contact employees?

In addition to answering the questions above, you should also refer to the success factors contributing to the effectiveness of this step. Please, therefore, turn to the grid "Top Management Commitment and Involvement Audit," which you will find at the end of Step 1, Part 2: A Seven-Step Audit for Attaining and Maintaining Customer Loyalty. Once you have completed these ratings, you will be ready to move on to the questions that relate to Step 2, Part 2.

Step 2

INTERNAL BENCHMARKING – ESTABLISHING A BASELINE

BACKGROUND INFORMATION

This step will help a company conduct an internal benchmarking study and establish a baseline for further improvement. The main categories of this study are as follows.

1. Measurement.
2. People.
3. Management.
4. Organization.
5. System.
6. Tools.
7. Design.
8. Suppliers.
9. Manufacturing.
10. Field Operations.
11. Support Services.

The questions that follow relate to each of these categories in turn.

QUESTIONS

1. Measurement

- Does the company's benchmarking measure:
  - ❏ customer loyalty
  - ❏ value added to core customers
  - ❏ cost of poor quality
  - ❏ cycle time?

Customer loyalty

- Are the number and percentage of loyal customers and their longevity assessed?

Value added to core customers

- Will this indicate money saved for core customers, as measured by them?

Cost of poor quality

- Will the cost of poor quality integrate the failings of:
  - ❏ management
  - ❏ human resources
  - ❏ products
  - ❏ services?

Note: Figure 6 in Step 2, Part 2: *A Seven-Step Audit for Attaining and Maintaining Customer Loyalty* depicts several elements associated with the cost of poor quality.

Cycle time

- Will the current cycle time for customer orders, new product introduction, manufacturing and key business processes such as accounts receivable and accounts payable be assessed?

2. People

- Will this be seen by the team as a significant assessment category?

Note: If a company devalues its employees, employees will pass this message on to the customers.

- In order to grow to their full potential, are employees:
  - ❏ listened to
  - ❏ supported
  - ❏ encouraged
  - ❏ trained
  - ❏ given opportunities?

- Does true empowerment mean giving them a piece of the action — administrative, managerial and financial?

3. Management

- Does the top management baseline include:
  - ❏ commitment
  - ❏ involvement
  - ❏ "walking the talk"
  - ❏ superordinate value
  - ❏ rewarding behaviors reinforcing customer service
  - ❏ demonstrating customer commitment by thought, word and deed?

4. Organization

- Will the company evaluate whether it is moving away from bureaucracy towards cross-functional teams such as:
  - ❏ development
  - ❏ new product development
  - ❏ customer order
  - ❏ others?

- Will it also assess whether the internal customer has been elevated to a position of importance, as scorekeeper and evaluator of the internal supplier's performance?

5. System

- Will the assessment in this category focus on whether policies and procedures exist for the good of the customer or for command and control by management?

- Will it also examine whether the old practices in hiring, training, evaluations, merit raises and promotion have been revolutionized to change the behavior and values of employees and move to a customer-focused culture?

6. Tools

Note: Tools have, traditionally, been a weak link in most companies and in many disciplines.

- Is there enough knowledge of tools to build up from a baseline level?

7. Design

- Is design of products and services governed by the "voice of the customer"?

- Or is it governed by the voice of the design engineer or management?

- Will the assessment include the extent to which there are design processes to achieve:
  - ❏ zero variation
  - ❏ zero field failures
  - ❏ minimal field service
  - ❏ built-in diagnostics
  - ❏ ergonomics
  - ❏ low cost
  - ❏ short cycle time?

8. Suppliers

- Will the baseline audit assess the same adherence to partnership principles as is done with customers, along with the amount and quality of active, concrete help rendered to each side?

9. Manufacturing

- Is it recognized that from the customer's perspective, there are two major elements associated with the effectiveness of manufacturing: quality and cycle time?

10. Field Operations

- Will the baseline assessment include:
  - ❏ packing
  - ❏ transportation
  - ❏ installation instructions
  - ❏ operating instructions
  - ❏ accuracy, completeness and timing of repair service?

THE CUSTOMER LOYALTY AUDIT

11. Support Services

- Is it understood that as product quality has steadily improved, customer dissatisfaction is increasingly centered on poor support service such as:
  - ❏ billing errors
  - ❏ wrong destinations
  - ❏ a run-around on inquiries
  - ❏ unsatisfactory problem resolution
  - ❏ lack of attention?

In addition to answering the questions above, you should also refer to the success factors contributing to the effectiveness of this step. Please, therefore, turn to the grid "Internal Benchmarking — Establishing A Baseline," which you will find at the end of Step 2, Part 2: A Seven-Step Audit for Attaining and Maintaining Customer Loyalty. Once you have completed these ratings, you will be ready to move on to the questions that relate to Step 3, Part 2.

Step 3

DETERMINING CUSTOMER REQUIREMENTS

BACKGROUND INFORMATION

This step focuses on several methods of determining customer requirements, including those that follow.

1. Market research.

2. Powerful tools for determining customer requirements.

3. Reading the customer's mind.

The questions below will help you to deal with each of these methods in turn.

QUESTIONS

1. Market Research

- Will the company use market research to determine customer requirements?

- Will one of the key questions of the research be: "What major experiences influenced your decision to try our product or service?"?

- Will the research establish why customers might have defected?

- Will research be undertaken as a team exercise?

2. Powerful Tools for Determining Customer Requirements

- Will these tools include:
  ❏ value research
  ❏ customer window model
  ❏ sensitivity analysis
  ❏ multi-attribute evaluation
  ❏ conjoint analysis
  ❏ quality function deployment?

Note: A further explanation of each of these tools can be found in Step 3, Part 2: *A Seven-Step Audit for Attaining and Maintaining Customer Loyalty*.

- Will the objectives of this study be to:
  - ❏ ascertain and prioritize customer requirements before a new design begins (in other words, capturing the voice of the customer rather than the voice of the engineer)
  - ❏ obtain the customer's view of the company's strengths and weaknesses, *vis-à-vis* its competition on each customer requirement
  - ❏ compare the company's strengths and weaknesses *vis-à-vis* its competition on each engineering specification, through reverse engineering (i.e. competitive analysis)
  - ❏ highlight incompatibilities in design (negative correlations)
  - ❏ as the bottom line, pinpoint the important, the new and the difficult in the preliminary design?

3. Reading the Customer's Mind

- Will it be established how a company really fathoms what's in customers' minds?

- Will it be established what their needs, expectations and requirements are?

Note: There are many techniques for this, but three very effective ones are:
- focus groups, clinics, panels
- customer contact personnel inputs
- one-on-one in-depth interviews.

Focus Groups, Clinics, Panels

- Will discussions be led by a trained facilitator or observed by key company personnel behind a one-way glass panel?

- Might the advantages be:
  - ❏ instant feedback
  - ❏ determination of consensus
  - ❏ diversity of opinions?

- Might the disadvantages be development of a "herd mentality" where a dominant person may pull the rest of the panel into a forced agreement or panel members may be hesitant to speak their true minds?

Customer Contact Personnel Inputs

- Will employees who frequently come into contact with customers be considered a very good source of information?

THE CUSTOMER LOYALTY AUDIT

One-On-One In-Depth Interviews

- Will interviews be conducted not only with people in a customer organization who make purchasing decisions, but also with actual users?

Note: These interviews should last around one to one-and-a-half hours.

- Will the interviewer let the customer describe — without structure or prompting at first — the key product or service attributes which would lead to increased purchases or cause purchases to decline?

- In some cases, might managers from the company conduct the interviews?

- In other cases, might outside support be preferable, using "blind" interviewers, not identified with a specific company, in order to get unbiased responses?

Note: Interviews generally continue until key responses are consistently repeated and until unique responses describe exceptional or unusual customers' responses. This is likely to happen after about 12 to 15 interviews.

The questions that follow will help the company not to repeat previous mistakes.

- Will research also poll former customers and non-customers in addition to existing and new customers?

- Might former customers, who have defected, provide a wealth of information about their disenchantment with the company?

- Might non-customers stipulate reasons they were never enticed to try the company's products or services?

- Will a concerted effort be made, using interviews, to touch these two important bases?

In addition to answering the questions above, you should also refer to the success factors contributing to the effectiveness of this step. Please, therefore, turn to the grid "Determining Customer Requirements," which you will find at the end of Step 3, Part 2: A Seven-Step Audit for Attaining and Maintaining Customer Loyalty. Once you have completed these ratings, you will be ready to move on to the questions that relate to Step 4, Part 2.

Step 4

ASSESSING THE CAPABILITIES OF COMPETITION

BACKGROUND INFORMATION

This step helps you to "know your enemy," in terms of your competition. It details a number of techniques, including those that follow, by which capabilities of the company's best competitor can be assessed and the gap in terms of customer satisfaction and loyalty quantified.

1. Quality function deployment (QFD).

2. Benchmarking.

3. Industry reports.

4. Independent laboratories.

The questions below will help you with each of these techniques in turn.

QUESTIONS

1. Quality Function Deployment (QFD)

- As a result of making comprehensive evaluations using the QFD matrix, will the company have a much clearer and more quantitative comparison of its strengths and weaknesses *vis-à-vis* competition?

Note: Evaluations are given in Step 4, Part 2: *A Seven-Step Audit for Attaining and Maintaining Customer Loyalty*.

2. Benchmarking

- As well as internal benchmarking, will competitive benchmarking and generic benchmarking also be used?

Note: Applied to the discipline of customer service, both of these additional benchmarking processes are in order.

Competitive Benchmarking

- Will this be able to determine who is the best competitor?

- Competitive benchmarking provides the advantage of directly comparing the customer service process between two companies with:

- ❏ similar products
- ❏ similar services
- ❏ similar customers.

- However, might the competitor benchmark company not cooperate in the study, regarding its customer service as highly proprietary?

Generic Benchmarking

- Will this be able to determine which is the best company (preferably with a non-competitor, which is possibly even better than a competitor)?

- Might generic benchmarking have the advantage of much easier access to and cooperation by the benchmark company, since it is not a competitor?

- Will both types of benchmarking be pursued, so the company gets two perspectives on best practices associated with customer service?

3. Industry Reports

- Will other important sources of competitive performances include the various reports published in the media such as:

  - ❏ J.D. Powers' reports on customer satisfaction
  - ❏ government reports
  - ❏ consumer magazines
  - ❏ commissioned studies?

- However, might consumer magazines have slants in their questionnaires, sample sizes, evaluation techniques and data shading?

4. Independent Laboratories

- Is there a danger that, although most of these render above-board service, the one who pays the piper gets to call the tune?

In addition to answering the questions above, you should also refer to the success factors contributing to the effectiveness of this step. Please, therefore, turn to the grid "Analyzing Capabilities of Competition," which you will find at the end of Step 4, Part 2: A Seven-Step Audit for Attaining and Maintaining Customer Loyalty. Once you have completed these ratings, you will be ready to move on to the questions that relate to Step 5, Part 2.

Step 5

MEASURING CUSTOMER SATISFACTION AND CUSTOMER LOYALTY

BACKGROUND INFORMATION

This step deals with the various methods (listed below) of measuring customer satisfaction as well as customer loyalty. At this point, you should refer to Step 5, Part 2: *A Seven-Step Audit for Attaining and Maintaining Customer Loyalty*, which explains the grading assigned to each matrix.

1. Customer satisfaction metrics (indirect measures).

2. Direct customer surveys.

3. Frequency of polling

4. Customer loyalty metrics.

The questions that follow relate to each of these methods in turn.

QUESTIONS

1. Customer Satisfaction Metrics — Indirect Measures

These include the following:

- *warranty costs*
- *customer complaints/claims*
- *market share*
- *cost of poor quality*
- *industry reports*
- *business statistics.*

Warranty Costs

- Does the company track its warranty costs?

- Is this done as a percentage of sales?

- Is the company aware that not only is this a catastrophic indication of customer dissatisfaction, it also comes too late?

Customer Complaints/Claims

- Instead of correcting problems, might the company hide behind excuses such as:
  - ❏ "no trouble found" where a failure could not be confirmed
  - ❏ customer misuse
  - ❏ customer's lack of knowledge in operating the product or service
  - ❏ customer fraud?

Note: These excuses are sleeping pills. When the company wakes up, it may well be out of business.

Market Share

- Is it understood that market share is not an accurate gauge of customer satisfaction and is even more nebulous as a gauge of customer loyalty?

Note: It measures the quantity, not the quality, of a company's services to its customers.

Cost of Poor Quality

- Is the company aware of this loss?
- Does the company estimate this loss?

Note: This can be an excellent metric if the cost of a defecting customer can be estimated, as outlined in Step 2, Part 2.

Business Statistics

- Will customer satisfaction be measured with business statistics:
  - ❏ for ratio of sales wins to sales losses
  - ❏ with capture ratios
  - ❏ for conversion efficiency
  - ❏ for mean time between winning a customer and losing that customer?
- Might the disadvantages of such business statistics be the numerous variables — hard to pinpoint as root causes — affecting customer satisfaction or dissatisfaction?

2. Direct Customer Surveys

- Will the best method for the company of measuring customer satisfaction be to ask the customers themselves for their evaluation?

Common to several techniques for this is the questionnaire. The next set of questions relates to questionnaire design dos and don'ts.

- Will the questionnaire be:
  - ❏ short
  - ❏ easy to fill out
  - ❏ user friendly?

- Will it take 15 minutes or less of the customer's time?

- Will the questions be:
  - ❏ unambiguous
  - ❏ easy to understand
  - ❏ easy to interpret?

- Will the questionnaire let customers, not managers, select the parameters important to them?

- Will there be a maximum of 10 to 15 parameters for the questionnaire, associated with those elements of customer satisfaction most important to customers?

- Will the questionnaire include truly important questions, such as:
  - ❏ "Would you buy this product or service again?"
  - ❏ "Would you buy a product of the same brand (i.e. other products made by the same company)?"
  - ❏ "Would you recommend this product (or service) to a friend?"
  - ❏ "How can we serve you better?"?

- Will there be time and space for responses?

- Will professionals with a proven track record (either within the company or outside consultants) be used to design the questionnaire?

- In telephone or person-to-person surveys, will trained interviewers who are sensitive to customers be used?

- Where possible, will outsiders be used?

Note: Customers are often more frank with them than with a company interviewer.

Other types of direct customer surveys include:

- *mail surveys*
- *telephone surveys*
- *focus groups, clinics, panels*
- *soliciting non-customer inputs*
- *soliciting former customer inputs*
- *customer-contact employee inputs*
- *one-on-one interviews*

Mail Surveys

- Might these be too impersonal?

- Might they provide only one-way communication and tend to be skewed towards complaining customers who may use the survey instrument to vent their feelings?

Note: While cheaper and quicker than other methods, these generate the poorest response from customers.

Telephone Surveys

- Might these provide two-way communications with the customer and allow emotional factors to be registered?

- Might the disadvantages be that:
  - targeted customers are often difficult to reach
  - the public is inundated with them and often resent them
  - the all-important body language signals are absent?

Soliciting Non-Customer Inputs

- Will asking non-customers how satisfied they are with various features and aspects of a competitor's products or services afford the company a benchmarking perspective?

- Will these inputs be valuable sources for improving the company's own performance?

Soliciting Former Customer Inputs

- Might the company miss a trick by not polling former customers to understand the reasons for their disenchantment?

- Might such encounters actually help in recapturing former customers?

Note: Focus groups, clinics and panels, customer-contact employee inputs and one-on-one interviews are all discussed in more detail in Step 3, Part 2.

3. Frequency of Polling

- Will the number of times customers are polled to determine satisfaction vary with different products and services and with different types of customers?

Note: A general rule of thumb is once per quarter. However, core customers need close and constant attention.

4. Customer Loyalty Metrics

- Will the measures for customer loyalty include:
  - ❏ a maintenance ratio
  - ❏ a defection rate
  - ❏ the amount and continuity of core customers
  - ❏ longevity of core customers
  - ❏ value to core customers?

In addition to answering the questions above, you should also refer to the success factors contributing to the effectiveness of this step. Please, therefore, turn to the grid "Measuring Customer Satisfaction and Loyalty," which you will find at the end of Step 5, Part 2: A Seven-Step Audit for Attaining and Maintaining Customer Loyalty. Once you have completed these ratings, you will be ready to move on to the questions that relate to Step 6, Part 2.

Step 6

ANALYZING CUSTOMER AND COMPETITIVE FEEDBACK

BACKGROUND INFORMATION

Once customer satisfaction and loyalty have been measured against customer requirements, feedback from customers, competition, former customers and non-customers should be analyzed. First, the pitfalls to these are covered. Then the following areas are looked at.

1. Developing a single customer satisfaction index.

2. Analysis of customer defections.

3. Analysis of non-customer buying habits.

4. Use of information technology.

5. The concentration decision.

The questions below will deal with each of these in turn.

QUESTIONS

The Pitfalls

- Might it be a pitfall sticking to a particular questionnaire, even though the response from customers is poor, inadequate or inappropriate?

- Might it be a pitfall not changing a survey format in order to track performance over time, even though the format needs to be revised and updated?

- Might it be a pitfall gathering so much data that you can't see the forest for the trees?

Note: Data pollution is a common weakness in many customer satisfaction surveys.

- Might it be a pitfall to have no follow-up?

- Might this be the worst scenario, caused by:
  ❏ disbelief in the data
  ❏ political infighting within the company
  ❏ lack of management support
  ❏ external conditions checkmating corrective action?

- Might it be a pitfall to use results incorrectly?

- Might it be a pitfall to combine "satisfied" and "very satisfied" ratings as a single measure of favorable customer responses?

1. Developing a Single Customer Satisfaction Index

- Is the elegance of the customer satisfaction index for your company the remarkable way in which it simultaneously analyzes:
  - ❏ the relative importance customers attach to their priority requirements
  - ❏ the strengths and weaknesses of the company *vis-à-vis* those requirements, as determined by the customer
  - ❏ the strengths and weaknesses of the company *vis-à-vis* its best competition, again as determined by the customer?

Note: A more detailed description of developing a single customer satisfaction index plus relevant figures is given in Step 5, Part 2.

2. Analysis of Customer Defections

- Is the company concerned only in a vague way about customer defections?

- Does the company measure its customer defection rates?

- Does it then analyze these rates for the main reasons for such defections?

Note: It is estimated that a 5 percent reduction in defections can result in an 85 percent increase in profit — a neglected gold mine!

3. Analysis of Non-Customer Buying Habits

- Does the company explore why various segments of the market do not buy its products or services but select its competitors instead?

- Might this type of benchmarking pay handsome dividends?

- Will it unearth causes such as:
  - ❏ little knowledge of the company or its products
  - ❏ poor quality and reliability as perceived by the public
  - ❏ poor public image
  - ❏ unfavourable mentions in the news media
  - ❏ product liability lawsuits and settlements
  - ❏ recall campaigns

THE CUSTOMER LOYALTY AUDIT

❏ disgruntled customers telling their friends and neighbors

❏ dealer sales representatives pushing competitors/ products or services?

4. Use of Information Technology (IT)

- Does the company use IT to allow a complete profile of each core customer, including:

  ❏ what products they buy

  ❏ where they buy

  ❏ others?

- Is this information used to provide various preferential services to reward the core customer, such as:

  ❏ advance information on sales

  ❏ discounts

  ❏ promotions?

5. The Concentration Decision

- Are there some customers that the customer would rather not keep?

- Might these include:

  ❏ dishonest customers, who take advantage of generous company policies

  ❏ dissatisfied customers, who complain perpetually regardless of the triviality of the complaint or the accommodation extended to them by the company

  ❏ customers who consistently seek to squeeze a company for price reductions without any redeeming characteristics to justify retaining them as customers

  ❏ other customers who only buy the tail-ends of a company's diversity of products or services in uneconomic quantities

  ❏ those who are not profitable to the company or unlikely to develop into preferred or core customers?

In addition to answering the questions above, you should also refer to the success factors contributing to the effectiveness of this step. Please, therefore, turn to the grid "Analyzing Customer and Competitive Feedback," which you will find at the end of Step 6, Part 2: A Seven-Step Audit for Attaining and Maintaining Customer Loyalty. Once you have completed these ratings, you will be ready to move on to the questions that relate to Step 7, Part 2.

Step **7**

CONTINUOUS IMPROVEMENT

BACKGROUND INFORMATION

This step concentrates on several facets, as outlined below, of a continuous improvement process.

1. Causes and remedies for typical customer complaints.

2. Management audits.

3. From freephone numbers to ombudsman to chief customer officer (CCO).

4. Statistics and lies.

5. Creative stimuli.

6. Business process reengineeering (BPR).

7. Customer contact employees.

The questions that follow deal with each of these facets in turn.

QUESTIONS

1. Causes and Remedies for Typical Customer Complaints

- Will customer complaints be divided into a few broad categories?

Note: Table 3 in Step 7, Part 2: *A Seven-Step Audit for Attaining and Maintaining Customer Loyalty* lists the most typical areas of customer problems, their causes and the most appropriate tools and techniques to correct them.

2. Management Audits

- Will a management audit be used to monitor and improve the effectiveness of services rendered to customers?

- Will these be:
  ❏ announced
  ❏ unannounced?

3. From Freephone Numbers to Ombudsman to Chief Customer Officer (CCO)

- Will the company facilitate linking up with customers through the use of freephone numbers, where customers can call in with their inquiries, concerns and complaints?

- To demonstrate their commitment to customers, will senior managers answer these freephone lines one day in a month?

Note: If they do, they will receive unfiltered feedback directly from customers, instead of the watered-down version fed to them by subordinates.

- Will the company appoint a senior executive as ombudsman to provide a master information center for customers who might otherwise get lost in a corporate maze?

Note: The ultimate is the appointment of a top management person as the company's CCO to be the customer's advocate in the entire corporation and to act as its "customer conscience."

- Will the CCO become second in importance only to the CEO?

- Will he or she marshal the company's entire customer activities, similar to a Chief Financial Officer covering all its financial matters?

4. Statistics and Lies

- Does the company use this discipline indiscriminately?

- Does it use design of experiments (DOE) to analzye and improve customer performance?

DOE is a powerful tool for preventing and solving product process problems. Among the variants or this technique are:

- *multivariate techniques*
- *paired comparisons.*

Multivariate Techniques

- Would the company consider using these to stratify families of variation in dealing with customers, such as:
    - ❏ geographic locations
    - ❏ product or service complexity
    - ❏ volume

❏ complaint categories
❏ salesforce competency
❏ time spent with customers
❏ others?

Paired Comparisons

- Would the company consider using these to ferret out repetitive differences in a number of characteristics associated with good customers and complaining customers?

5. Creative Stimuli

- Will other tools used to improve customer performance include:
  ❏ brainstorming
  ❏ force field analysis
  ❏ value engineering?

Brainstorming

- Will this be based on the premise of the worth of the final ideas for improvement being directly proportional to the number of ideas in an initial brainstorming session?

Force Field Analysis

- Will this systematically plan measures to enhance driving forces and simultaneously attenuate the restraining forces to achieve a much improved level of performance?

Value Engineering

- Applied to any process or service that affects customers, will it ask:
  ❏ "What does it do?"
  ❏ "What is the function of the process?"
  ❏ "What does it cost?"
  ❏ "What else can perform the function (with improved performance?"
  ❏ "What will that cost (at a lower cost)?"?

Note: The improved process is generally a radical departure from the current one. Another facet of value engineering is asking the "5 Whys" as listed in Step 7, Part 2.

6. Business Process Reengineering (BPR)

- Will the company adopt BPR techniques such as:
  - ❏ cross-functional teams
  - ❏ flow charting
  - ❏ "out-of-box" thinking?

- Will these be adopted through evolution rather than undertaking a full blown revolution?

Cross-Functional Teams

- Will these be utilized to convert what might be a bureaucratic, vertical organization into a hard-hitting horizontal, interdisciplinary team to improve business processes and focus on customers?

Flow Charting

- Will cross-functional teams use flow charting to map every step in the business process, starting with the customer and going back to the start of the process?

Note: Flow charting is also known as process mapping.

"Out-of-Box" Thinking

- Will "out-of-box" thinking be used to jettison the entire process, flow chart and all?

7. Customer-Contact Employees

The questions below will help you to determine how best to empower the company's customer-contact employees.

- Will selection/hiring be based on sensitivity to customers, team playing abilities and innovative potential?

- Will compensation be commensurate with the importance of interface with customers?

- Will training deal not only with a thorough knowledge of products and services, but also with skills in listening, innovation and defusing customer frustration and anger?

- Will decision making include the ability to change rules and regulations from those serving the company to those serving the customer and capture their satisfaction and loyalty?

THE CUSTOMER LOYALTY AUDIT

- Will morale be continually assessed through management and customer surveys?

- Will recognition by management for outstanding service to customers become a way of life?

- Will this recognition include bonuses and other rewards, along with celebrations for the entire team?

In addition to answering the questions above, you should also refer to the success factors contributing to the effectiveness of this step. Please, therefore, turn to the grid "Continuous Improvement," which you will find at the end of Step 7, Part 2: A Seven-Step Audit for Attaining and Maintaining Customer Loyalty.

IN CONCLUSION ...

All of the questions listed in this section will hopefully help you to plan an audit that will establish customer loyalty. The extensive explanations for each of the seven steps given in Part 2: *A Seven-Step Audit for Attaining and Maintaining Customer Loyalty* will help you to answer these questions to best effect.

Good luck!

Parts 1 and 2: Keki R. Bhote *is the President of Keki R. Bhote Associates, a company specializing in Quality and Productivity Improvement. He has consulted with over 300 companies all over the world, ranging from diverse manufacturing and service industries to universities and governments. He has retired from Motorola, where he was Senior Corporate Consultant on Quality and Productivity Improvement. He played a key role in Motorola winning the prestigious* Malcolm Baldrige National Quality Award – *the first company to win the honor as a total corporation – and in launching its renowned* Six Sigma *process for continuous quality improvement. He is still a Consultant Emeritus with Motorola.*

Part 3 *has been adapted from* The Company AuditGuide *published by Cambridge Strategy Publications Ltd.* **Part 4** *has been developed by Cambridge Strategy Publications Ltd.*